GETTING INTO

before the

Performing Arts

SECOND EDITION

EMMA CAPREZ

TROTMAN

Getting into Performing Arts
This second edition published in 2002
by Trotman & Company Ltd
2 The Green, Richmond, Surrey TW9 1PL

© Trotman & Company Limited 2002

British Library Cataloguing in Publication Data
A catalogue record for this book is available from the
British Library

ISBN 0 85660 834 3

Typeset by Palimpsest Book Production Limited,
Polmont, Stirlingshire
Printed and bound in Great Britain
by Creative Print & Design (Wales) Ltd

CONTENTS

ABOUT THE AUTHOR

Emma Caprez studied for her BA in Design and Media Management at Thames Valley University. For her final-year project she researched, wrote and illustrated a book on the history of the Ealing School of Art and organised a follow-up exhibition and reunion. She graduated with First Class Honours in 1993. She has worked on other research projects including one on the feasibility of drama therapy for disabled people with the First Chance Project. She has written several children's books as well as writing for two international music papers *Rumba* and the *LA Rock Review*. She has had photographs published in *Melody Maker* and contributed towards university literature. Emma researched and wrote the book *Getting into the Media*, and produced the video of the same name. She edited Trotman's flagship title, *The Disabled Students' Guide to University* and lives with her partner and two children in London.

ACKNOWLEDGEMENTS

Very special thanks to Rook Randle, Biba Maya Petal and Suky Ella Lupin for their understanding and support. A special thank you also to Arlette Caprez for her help in researching the Directory and her support. Also to Peach and Maisie Kazen, Pops, Mandy and Jamila Prowse, Sophie, Per, Paula and Oskar Kviman, Clare Pace, Sophie and Sasha Struth, Juliette Preston, Alan, Cyan and Cal Stuart and Lynn and Poppy Towers.

A big thank you to Rachel Lockhart and Amanda Williams at Trotman.

A huge thank you to Stewart Wright for contributing such a thought-provoking and entertaining Foreword.

Per Kviman, RCA; Lucy Butler, dance student; Della, dancer and dance teacher; Martin Brown, Equity; Sarah Bullimore, The Place Dance Services; Marguerite Porter, Royal Ballet; Christian Wright, Abbey Road Studios; Annie Carpenter, Actor; Eve Delves, MTV UK; Nancy Cleary, Arts Council of England; Peter Fordham, Musicians' Union; Adrian McKinney, Itchy Teeth Records; Anna Maratos-Tooth, British Society of Music Therapists; Tim Delaney, Polygram; Gabriella Meara, Actor; Marcia Bennie, The Orange Tree Theatre; Gunilla Karlson, GT Management; Jeff Dray, tour manager; Matthew Napier, BBC Children's Drama; Alex Scannel, Abbey Road Studios; Marc Wooton, Karen Adams and Alison Bullock, The Orange Tree Theatre; Rachel Lacey, Tennant Artists; Pedro Machado, CandoCo; Caroline Giles, Yorkshire Television; Ian Harvey, Focus Management; Toby Sergeant, Press Office Department of Culture, Media and Sport; Edward Birch and Rowan M Dorey, Arts Council of England; Josephine Leask, dance critic; Sarah Matthews and Toby Smith, Central School of Ballet; Suzie Leighton, Dance UK; Tim McGee, Metier; Catherine Willmore, The Place Dance Services.

FOREWORD

By Stewart Wright (Actor)

A burlesque of Rudyard Kipling's *If.*

(If) You Want To Be A Performer

If *you can keep your job when all about you*
Are losing theirs and blaming it on you;
If you can keep your faith when the business doubts you,
But make allowance for their doubting too;
If you can wait and not be tired by waiting,
Or being lied to, don't deal in lies,
Or being slated, don't give way to slating,
And yet don't get too down, nor into highs;

If *you can dream – and not make dreams your master;*
If you can act – yet not make it your aim;
If you can cope with 'darling, funnier and faster'
And resist temptation to go insane;
If you can bear the stress of reviews pending
Both Good and Bad they're a trap for fools,
Or watch the career you gave your life to ending
And stoop and reinvent with worn out tools:

If you can make one heap of all your courage
And risk it on a profession such as this,
And fail, and start again at your beginning
And never breathe a word unless you're sloshed;
If you can force your heart and nerve and soul
To serve the turn long after they are gone.
And so hold on when nothing's left at all
Except the will which says to them 'You're on!'

If you can talk with Parky – and keep your virtue,
Or walk with stars – nor lose the common touch,
If neither 'no's' nor commissioners' trends can hurt you,
If you can hype yourself but not too much
If we had only one minute
And the stage you'd chosen for your existence,
Apart from luck or a catchphrase 'in it'
By George
What you'll need is per-sis-tence!

Stewart Wright's credits include the leading man in the BBC drama series *Rescue Me*, with Sally Phillips, and *Wild West* with Dawn French. He also appeared in *All My Sons*, at the National, the film *Bridget Jones' Diary*, and the BBC's *People Like Us*.

PREFACE

If you are ambitious to achieve a career in music, drama or dance, chances are (particularly if you want to be a performer) you will have already taken the first steps and learned to play an instrument, joined a drama group or have been attending dance classes since you were very young.

You may have already experienced how fierce the competition is and realised you need more than just talent to carry you through. Having an understanding of how the business operates as well as possessing a range of skills relevant to your chosen career can be a massive advantage.

If you have the ability to conceive a vision of what you are about to achieve and if you truly believe that no obstacles, knockbacks or hardships will break that vision, then all you need is the right training, skills and advice to power it.

Getting into Performing Arts will provide you with case studies which give personal insights from people working within the performing arts, as well as a list of job functions, types of training available and a very comprehensive directory. It will give you an understanding of what the industry is really like and suggest ways of seeking employment.

In a rapidly changing industry, with a public hungry to be entertained, it's out there waiting for you to get it and give it – good luck.

Rook Randle

Songwriter and Musician

INTRODUCTION

The need to experience the arts is fundamental to our quality of life, and the performing arts play a very important part in this. Without music, drama or dance our lives would be severely deprived – they are an intrinsic part of our cultural existence, and the pleasure derived from taking part in them leads many people to desperately want to make the performing arts a valid career option.

THE PERFORMING ARTS

The performing arts industry – the collective name for music, drama and dance – is notoriously competitive, insecure and breaks a lot of hearts. Yet for thousands of people this is the only business they've ever wanted to get into. You only have to look around you to see examples of celebrity successes who've made their mark on the entertainment world; Kylie Minogue, Denzel Washington and Darcy Bussell. There are now even programmes, which attract huge audiences, dedicated to creating stars, such as *Pop Idol*'s Will Young. But these are the lucky ones, the ones who have inspired you, given you the determination and ambition to get in the business and become a success. But for every one success there are many more who have just received another rejection letter, or who've just failed yet another audition. So how do you improve your chances and what is success?

What is success?

Success in the entertainment world is not about being rich and famous. It's about securing work in an industry that you love being part of. It's about enjoying what you do for a living. Success doesn't mean being in constant employment either – for a performer that is rarely the case. The majority are freelance, which means none of the usual perks of full employment such as holiday and sick pay or maternity benefit and pension schemes. The reality for many people working in the performing arts, particularly the performers, is a succession of short-term contracts, for dancers the expenses of continual training and fitness regimes, and low levels of income. Progressively more performers leave their training with student debts, work for the minimum wage, and eventually may not be entitled to a state pension.

Four out of five freelance actors will be 'resting' or out of acting work at any one time, and just because you've had some acting work doesn't mean you will instantly secure some more. You may have to wait several months or a year, or more, before something else comes up. Alternatively you may not have any work for years and then suddenly start working. It is not a predictable business. For dancers as well, learning to survive between contracts is a skill, as is finding more work. Many people working in the performing arts industry will need to rely on Jobseeker's Allowance (JSA) as a source of income during these periods of being without a job, though securing this benefit may also prove difficult if you are seen to be self-employed. Trade unions, such as Equity, can help you with benefit applications when in between work.

Long hours

The working day for those in music, drama and dance may be as long as twelve hours and the majority of employment is based in London where those intent on a career in these industries flock to. Finding out the streets of London are *not* paved with gold is still a disillusionment to many.

Rejection

All performers must face rejection, whether it be from a record company, a theatre or a dance company, so it is vital to have the strength of character and tenacity to carry on. Belonging to an organisation such as the Musicians' Union (MU), Equity, The Place Dance Services (listed in the Directory at the end of this book) or having an agent can help give you the vital support you need. Indeed, actors will find it almost impossible to get paid work without a reputable agent, but getting an agent and getting work requires something more than talent. All performers must have self-promotional skills. Talent on its own is unlikely to get you work. You need to market yourself and your talent so agents and employers want you. Training courses often help you attain these skills.

'If you look in any of the casting magazines such as *PCR (Production and Casting Report)* and apply, they will say "Great, have you got an agent?" and as soon as you say "No," they're not interested. To get an agent they have to see you in something to know you can act. So in order to get into acting you need an agent and in order to get an agent you need to be in something.'
Alice Brickwood, Actor

Length of career

The working life of an actor can go on indefinitely and as many actors drop out by their thirties it becomes less competitive the older you get, but the pop musician and the dancer have a shorter working life. The dancer will rarely work past his or her mid-thirties and the pop musician is unlikely to be taken up by a record company after he or she has reached their mid- to late twenties. It is necessary, therefore, to ensure you have gained qualifications that will help you find another career after your performance one has terminated, whether that be in a related occupation or not.

Qualifications and work experience

Not all people wanting to get into the performing arts will choose to perform, wanting to go into administrative, managerial, therapeutic or teaching occupations. These are equally competitive. Find out what qualifications you need and get some training that relates to the area of work you want to pursue. Students are now required to help support themselves financially throughout their higher education. This means Student Loans and Career Development Loans are often needed, but those involved with the insecure and irregular work pattern typical of the performing arts lifestyle may find it particularly difficult to pay them back.

Getting qualifications is important, but getting experience – paid or voluntary – is vital, even for the lowest level of jobs. Prospective employers are going to be more likely to take you on if you have evidence of prior experience such as helping out backstage, managing a local band or helping a dance company with publicity. It not only demonstrates your commitment to the industry, but also your initiative and ability.

> 'I think the fact I had done a year's voluntary work during which time I had spent one day a week at college doing my City and Guilds in electronics was enough to show I had initiative and an aptitude for wanting to learn.' *Alex Scannel, Engineer, Abbey Road Studios*

A knowledge of the industry

Having a knowledge of the industry is important too. Go to concerts and theatre productions. Read the relevant press and visit relevant websites. Find out the different work opportunities that exist. Get to know the important names, companies and organisations and talk to anyone who can help you, whether it be for advice or to offer you a useful connection (and don't forget to always have business cards to give out – you never know when you might need them). The music business, in particular, rarely recruits employees externally. People tend to be employed through contacts (nepotism is rife), recommendation or in-house, so getting your foot in the door is vital.

CURRENT STATE OF THE INDUSTRY

Funding

Funding of the arts is always a huge area of concern with many theatres, dance companies or support organisations unable to operate without it. The Department of Culture, Media and Sport funds the arts industry through the Arts Council of England who distribute grant-in-aid and Lottery funds to arts organisations both directly and via the Regional Arts Boards. Funding for the arts in Scotland, Wales and Northern Ireland is via the Scottish Arts Council, the Arts Council of Wales and the Arts Council of Northern Ireland. Consequently, Arts Councils are able to decide what and who to support without Government intervention.

In 2001 there was a rise in the level of arts funding and by 2003/4 there will be an average 17 per cent rise in funding for the Arts Council's regularly funded organisations, which include companies such as the Dance Trust and Generator (see Directory). The Arts Council's grant-in-aid budget will rise by nearly £100 million to £337 million in 2003/4. This can only be good news for the performing arts and the people seeking to work in them as well as those who already do.

Greater participation

In 1999, Chris Smith, the then Minister for Culture, Media and Sport, challenged the arts sector to increase participation in the UK arts from half to two-thirds of the population.

As a result, the Department for Culture, Media and Sport (DCMS) has set out ten goals to make the arts more accessible, including: innovation, a thriving arts sector, more consumption and more participation in the arts, better use of arts in education and combating social exclusion and promoting regeneration.

Audience levels

Audiences for West End theatres fluctuate all the time, however it was widely believed that the events of 11 September did have an impact on attendance numbers. At their lowest point in the weeks following 11 September, audiences had fallen by 13.9 per cent compared to the same week in the previous year. Audiences have since recovered but can fluctuate for no apparent reason. *Peggy Sue Got Married* closed in the period after 11 September, but it is not certain whether this was directly related as shows often close early, even when West End audiences are strong.

While the general popularity of West End productions means a large number of people can be employed, theatre, film and television do tend to use big names to play lead roles so are less likely to take risks by using new actors. This makes it very hard for actors to break into the industry. Theatre tends to typically attract a middle-class audience so there is a need to encourage more popular support as advocated by the DCMS.

Encouraging new and younger audiences by the use of SMS text messaging is what Sadler's Wells hopes to do. This is the first theatre in the UK to adopt this method, a strategic marketing tool, to enable customers to use their mobile phones to book tickets.

The Royal Opera House also reports that there is a new audience coming to see performances, and so boosting audience numbers, as a result of advertising, including over the Internet. A large majority of first-timers include students or young people earning less than £30,000 a year. The cheaper seats cost £50, more expensive than those of their more heavily subsidised European counterparts, and more expensive than West End theatres. Wider access to opera has been helped along by a big screening of a live relay of *Romeo and Juliet* in Victoria Park, with similar events to take place outside London.

ISRC

Technological developments mean that music is available online, with predicted sales of music being accessed this way reaching around $4 billion by 2004. The International Standard Recording Code (ISRC) is a means of identifying all sound and audio-visual recordings internationally. Each ISRC is a unique and permanent way of identifying a specific recording which acts as a permanent digital fingerprint, encoded into a product. This means that when the recorded music is broadcast and electronically transmitted it can be automatically identified, so playing a significant role in copyright legislation of digital transmission for music and devices and formats, such as DVD.

Technological development

The advancement in technology has helped improve box office, lighting and sound systems as well as aiding design for theatre by using computers. The Internet can also aid in picking up business as a place where people book their tickets. It has also opened new media for performers. Live performances can now be integrated into computer programs and software which means interactive producers are opting for humans to replace computer generated characters.

Technological advancement has also meant you don't have to be trained in music or be able to play an instrument anymore because you can create from other people's music by using samples and computers. In fact you don't even have to sing that well either as your voice can be altered by technology. You don't even have to be a person anymore – in Japan they have created a 3D hologram image singer who doesn't even exist. They've also created a 3D Elvis who does gigs!

Even dance is able to utilise technology, as evidenced in the Arts Council of England's new dance-for-screen productions, *Capture*, which use film, video, DVD and computers, demonstrating the potential of existing and emergent technology in this genre.

New methods of casting

Advanced technology has even provided help for casting directors. In March 2002, *Spotlight*, famous casting directories for actors, signed a three-year deal with the BBC to use *Spotlight*'s online casting resource, *Spotlight Casting Live*. The online resource has an award-winning search engine and means that BBC programme makers and casting directors will be able to search for actors matching their necessary criteria – such as black female, tall, horserider – with great ease and speed.

There is no doubt that technology and the digital age has had, and will continue to have, an immense effect on the performing arts industry, both in its production and how it is viewed. It is necessary to keep up with these constant changes so you can keep yourself in the picture, get yourself in training and work, and be involved at the forefront of change in this hugely exciting industry. With hard work, dedication, enthusiasm, networking and a certain amount of good fortune you may just make it.

Organisations

There are various organisations which may be of help to your career in the performing arts and these are listed in the Directory for your perusal, including the Musicians' Union (MU), Equity and The Place Dance Services. It is worth checking this section to see if any of them can offer you any useful information, advice or support. Check the Directory for other relevant organisations, publications and useful addresses.

Chapter 1
MUSIC

Music is one of the UK's largest, most dynamic and constantly evolving industries, which contributes more than £3 billion annually to the UK economy. The UK's performance in music has an estimated share of around 10–15 per cent in the world market and is the third biggest market for music sales in the world, and second as a source of repertoire.

The All-Party Music Group has been formed by representatives from the music industry with MPs and peers, to create a better understanding within parliament of this important industry.

Competition

Of all the performing arts genres, music is the most competitive. Year on year, school leavers, graduates and others wishing to leave a nine-to-five existence look to the music industry in the hope they can build a career. Getting into the business, however, takes a lot of hard work, dedication and determination. It is an extremely competitive business with more than 100,000 people working in the industry. The Musicians' Union, the second largest union of musicians in the world, has 31,000 members.

Youth market

'I am in the studio until after 10pm twice a week, as we have a live show broadcast in the evening. If I'm not in the studio I'm attending gigs, album launch events or out with record labels. I start work about 10am. I put in the hours as the work demands. If I need to work seven days a week 14 hours a day – I will. Work is my social life. Sad eh? I eat, sleep, live and breathe my work.'
Eve Delves, Talent and Artist Relations Manager

Music is created and bought – in the main – by young people and this is reflected in the industry, where the majority of positions are filled by people aged 20 to 40. A long working day, followed by after-work business when gigs, launches, media events and dinners have to be attended, means that people in the music business have very little outside social life.

Job insecurity

It may seem like a glamorous life but the pay, particularly at the outset, can be very poor and jobs insecure. Even the people at the top, particularly those in A&R (artists and repertoire), have little job security – their jobs are on the line if the artists they sign don't reach the level of success expected of them. In other words, they are only as good as the last hit record they worked on. This is equally valid for the artists themselves, with bands no longer being developed over a long period of time. More than ever before you will find 'one hit wonders' – artists who have one successful song and who you never hear of again.

Live music threatened

The Musicians' Union has been campaigning against the use of pre-recorded music which has become increasingly popular with pantomimes throughout the UK. This of course decreases job opportunities for thousands of musicians at Christmas, which they have previously relied on as an important part of their financial security.

Most major venues are now owned by big companies, which means it is harder for new acts to play them. Some venues actually require the artists to pay *them* to play.

Reaching success

Being signed by a record and/or publishing company is considered reaching a modicum of success amongst artists, but the road to getting there is a long, dusty one with lots of potholes. Now, with music companies being run by accountants who favour playing safe rather than taking risks, the industry seems to work to a formula, producing more manufactured bands such as Westlife and Hear'say.

An early start

It is likely that classical musicians will have started learning an instrument in childhood with formal lessons. Pop musicians on the other hand may not have started on their musical career quite so early, but both are highly competitive industries and require talent, hard work – all musicians must practise regularly – and a certain amount of making yourself heard in the right place at the right time. Classical musicians will put a lot of preparation and effort into entering competitions such as the ones put on by the schools of music and the BBC. (Refer to the *British Music Yearbook* for more details. See Directory.) Winning these will provide the musicians with a respect and reputation that can be very helpful to their careers. But achieving recognition is not easy or glamorous. Touring and spending long periods away from home, often in grotty guest houses, and travelling in the back of a shabby van can be a dismal experience. Pay is low and second jobs are often needed in order to stay financially afloat, but at least, unlike the actor, it is possible to have a secondary career – working during the day and gigging and rehearsing at night. Professional musicians are generally self-employed, so don't get the usual perks of fully employed status.

Perks

There are many perks to working in the music business, such as free entry to show and backstage parties, complimentary CDs and maybe having dinner with artists you admire. Above all you have the satisfaction of working in the industry that produces what you love – music.

CASE STUDY

Christian Wright, CD Preparation Engineer, Abbey Road Studios

What made you become interested in the music business?

'Ever since playing music as a teenager, music has been a big part of my life. I have been in bands since I was 14. I went to a lot of gigs and still do. At 18 I got a job in my local music venue behind the bar while I was studying for my A-levels. I got a break when the in-house engineer couldn't do one night and I was asked to look after the touring engineer for that band. Unfortunately the band's touring engineer didn't turn up, forcing me to get thrown in at the deep end. Fortunately it went well, the promoter was chuffed enough to give me a once-a-week job at the venue as an engineer.'

What relevant training did you do?

'After A-levels I spoke to a friend who worked at Air Studios. He suggested that work experience would give me the same chance of getting into studios as going to university. I decided to take on the advice and sent out 50 CVs. I took extreme care with the presentation of my CV and it arrived at the right time and right place regarding Abbey Road. I started in the copy rooms of Abbey Road three years ago when I was 19 and got promoted to my current post of CD Preparation Engineer a year and a half later. My employer was looking for someone to train and not just a specifically qualified person.'

How successful is your band?

'I don't really get paid for my work as a musician. We are still trying to get signed and recently got ourselves a manager. We get paid OK money when we play London venues (Water Rats/Monarch). However, in proportion to the amount we pay out in practice studios, equipment and travel, until we are signed there's no money to earn – unless I become a pub rock-covers band singer and start playing weddings or karaoke prize nights. When that happens I hope I will be at least 50 and have decided that shame is inevitable.

'In my band, Luxor, I have to work with other people. I don't believe one person's musical ideas are enough to carry them into the music industry from an artistic angle. I have to work with friends who I trust and have absolute faith in. Not necessarily the same musical influences, maybe some similar influences, but the most important factor is how we work together both musically and in personality. It took me five years to find a band that I'm really happy about.'

How has the music industry changed since you first began to work in it?

'The downloadable angle of the music industry has made it an even tougher place to get along. The money isn't there as much as it was and most aspects of the music industry are scaling down. Many companies are also leaving the industry altogether as it is too competitive to survive.'

Do you belong to any relevant organisations or unions?

'No, something I haven't needed as yet, but should look at more. I feel I'm astute enough now and I have absolute faith and trust in our manager to do the best thing for us. I also make sure I know everything that is going on and keep updated as much as possible. This would get harder if success occurs, but that is when you have to surround yourself with the right people, treat them well and always be aware that there are evil people out there in every industry, with the music industry having a high proportion.'

Jeff Dray, Tour Manager for Coldplay

Jeff Dray's entry into the music business may sound comical, but in fact is not that far from typical. His friend's band was going on tour and he took time off from his painting and decorating job to see them play. After falling asleep on their tour bus he ended up waking in Manchester and was forced to help out. He didn't think too much about it until some friends in a different band needed some help, and knowing of his previous escapade asked him to assist them.

'It all progressed from there really. I kept getting more work. I got all my work through contacts. You're on the road working and you bump into other bands and they see you doing a good job and you give them your phone number. They remember you and next time they need someone they call you and ask you to work for them.'

So you didn't plan to work in the music business?

'No, it just happened. Everyone I knew was a wannabe musician so when they started getting some success I'd help out. At first I didn't get much – maybe a beer and then £30 a night and then I started to think, "Hold on, maybe I could make a career out of this". I started off doing backline (looking after equipment and tuning guitars etc.) and driving. You either do one or the other or both depending on the level of the band. Then after a couple of years I tour-managed a band called Daisy Chainsaw.'

How did you come to tour manage Coldplay?

'I gave up touring at the end of 1998. I had done four tours back-to-back and I was burnt out. I ran a restaurant for a while, then in June 1999 Coldplay's manager called and asked me to work for them. I had been recommended to them by their lawyers. I refused their offer, but they called me again the next day saying I had been recommended to them again, this time by their record label. They told me they couldn't get anyone else so I said I'd help out. By 2000 they had got very busy and I began working for them full-time. I have been working for them ever since.'

What does your work as a tour manager entail?

'I put together the tour budget, organise hotels, crew, transport, equipment hire and anything else necessary to make the tour happen. Before the tour starts I speak with the promoters – this is called "advancing the tour" – to make sure everything is organised. I have to sort out the basic contract – concerning the financial requirements – and then I have to check we have the necessary "riders" – these are things extra to the basic contract and include the drinks and food we will need plus the "tech rider" to make sure we have the PA needed and so on. On tour I am responsible for the monies – collecting and paying – ensuring the band are looked after, checking in and out of hotels and just generally being responsible for any problems such as equipment breakdown, hiring alternative equipment and transport, dealing with artist problems. When I was working with a previous band, I had to take an artist to hospital for collapsing on tour. Basically you have to be a combination of a diplomat and a tyrant because you have to make sure everything happens on time, which means dragging people out of bed when they don't want to get up. After the tour I have to get the accounts together. This means getting the receipts for fuel and hotels etc. to present back to the management or record company, depending on who you are dealing with.'

Advice?

'Get into music at a local level. Hang out with local musicians and at local venues and learn as much as you can. Don't be frightened to ask questions – I'm still learning even now – learn to drive, and be prepared to work for peanuts.'

ATTRIBUTES

Relevant qualities for those wishing to work in the music business are listed below.

Look at the list and see if you have the necessary attributes for a job in the music business.

- Creativity
- Self-confidence
- Sociability
- Stamina
- Tenacity
- Level-headedness
- Broadmindedness
- Enthusiasm
- Knowledge of music
- Good communication skills
- Organisational skills
- Computer literacy
- Ability to work well under pressure.

Qualifications (particularly a degree if you want to pursue a career in the classical side of the music business) are a good asset, but work experience is essential and above all you will need a genuine love of music, because without that you will not survive what is a very tough and cut-throat business.

The Biz

Per Kviman, A&R Manager, RCA

Per became interested in following a career in music after discovering bands such as Kiss, Black Sabbath, Sex Pistols as well as Ebba Gron, a band from Per's native country, Sweden. While still at school, Per spent money from the pupil council (the Swedish equivalent of a students' union) on bringing in bands to play in his home town of Vaxholm. His involvement in setting up gigs led him to become a volunteer journalist for a bi-weekly music magazine, comically titled *Schlager*, which means 'Eurovision Song Contest', but which was actually more along the lines of *NME* (*New Musical Express*).

'I was 16 then and I got frustrated with writing about bands that didn't have any record deals and so couldn't get exposure. My friend, Lars, and I decided to start up our own record label. It was all self-financed through short-term loans from the bank. Through this company I started working with a guy called Harry who worked from the UK with me in Sweden. We got independent distribution to access Europe and from 1984 to 1990 looked after five or six acts such as Leather Nun, 13 Moons and All That Jazz. We also imported British records by bands such as The Mission, Play Dead, Pop Will Eat Itself – a lot of Rough Trade records. Most of the Leather Nun records gave us a profit and we licensed a few of our bands to major labels in America. In 1988 Harry started working for Arista and my label was sold to MVG. MVG asked me to run Wire Records and so I had bands like Clawfinger and Backyard Babies. In 1994 I started a management company to manage a lot of these bands and I also had someone else to work from an office in New York so we were taking care of Scandinavia and North America. In 1998 Harry hired me to work for RCA as an A&R Manager, which is when I came to the UK. I signed Shea Seger and worked with Hymn from Finland and Backyard Babies, Waterboys and Skindread.'

What criteria are essential to you in order to be interested in an act?

'They must have that star quality, even more than the songs, because you can always work with the songs. The star aura is really important, they must be interesting to look at and have a lot of attitude – they don't have to be nice – and in the end, good songs.'

What are the pros and cons of working in the music industry?

'The pros are that you can really push for music that you really like yourself and make a difference and, of course, working in music. The cons are that music sometimes becomes too much of a job rather than fun. There is also too much politics in the music business as a whole.'

How has the music industry changed since you've worked in it?

'It has become very conservative, very safe, not enough risks are taken. It is good that there are more music outlets, e.g. *Kerrang TV* and new TV channels helping rock music which would otherwise be blocked in mainstream programming. A lot of the great grunge music of the early 90s which had success in America never broke over in the UK because they didn't have the media support they needed here in the UK.'

Any advice?

'Dare to be yourself. Push the limit and dare to do something which stands out. Go for it, don't hold back. Do whatever it takes and *don't* try and do it if you can't.'

Genres

For the simplification of this book, music has been divided into two genres – classical and every other type, referred to collectively as 'pop'. To avoid confusion orchestras, soloists, bands etc. are referred to collectively as 'artists'.

THE JOBS

The personal attributes and skills listed under each job description are in addition to those highlighted in the previous section.

Performers – classical and popular

Performers produce music either via an instrument or vocally. Instruments, other than electronic, belong to five main families: percussion, strings, brass, keyboard and woodwind. Classical performers – both musicians and opera singers – are nearly always trained either at a music college or university. They are generally freelance and play in ensembles, chamber groups, orchestras or as soloists. Singers may be part of a choir, opera singers or soloists. Some classical musicians will have agents, particularly if they are soloists. Pop musicians and/or vocalists may be self-taught without any formal training. They may work as part of a group or as a solo artist. Music is also created by using samples of other people's work and computer-generated material, in which case you would not necessarily need to know how to play any instruments at all (see Remixer, below), although it is an art to construct this kind of music. This category of music making could also come under the role of a producer. Work includes: concerts, recording, videos, television and radio, session work and touring. For pop artists, image is all important. Front people need:

- Star quality
- Talent
- Dedication
- Self-discipline
- Ability to work as part of a team
- Ability to accept constructive criticism
- Ability to sight-read (classical)
- Ambition
- Necessary skills/training if applicable.

Composers and songwriters

Composers and songwriters write part or all of the music piece including the lyrics, where applicable. They may work independently or in a team and may or may not be the person who performs the work. Dependent on the kind of market they are targeting, they must recognise what is commercially viable if a recording contract is their aim, or what is unique enough for the publishing company to risk taking on. The composer or songwriter is the person who makes the most money when a record becomes a hit. You need:

- Musical ability
- Ability to be objective about your own work
- Dedication.

Remixer

Songs can be remixed by using samples from the original (e.g. a repetitive hookline) and combining these with new beats and loops to create a completely new version, generally using some of the original lyrics with new additional ones. Most remixers are DJs with dance music backgrounds who are brought in to remix an artist's tracks to broaden their appeal. You need:

- Initiative
- Technical knowledge.

Working in multimedia

Sound technicians and musicians work in the ever-growing field of multimedia to marry sound to the visuals and textual information presented in the package. Multimedia companies will often commission specialist musicians who are highly skilled in composing suitable 'bites'. The musicians will generally have knowledge and experience of sound recording. You need:

- Musical ability
- Technical knowledge and experience.

Conductor

The conductor is responsible for conveying to the players or orchestra the beat, metre, dynamics and expression of the music. S/he does this by using a baton, which is waved in the air to indicate to the players what is required of them. As well as being able to sight-read, conductors are generally experienced musicians, although it is possible to enter the profession directly. Some orchestras offer traineeships for young people wishing to work with an experienced conductor and learn the ropes. The conductor is usually the one who rehearses the orchestra and chooses the music to be played. The conductor may also introduce the music to the audience. You need:

- Musical skills
- Excellent sense of rhythm
- Experience.

Artist/band/orchestral manager

The manager works for the artist to secure and negotiate recording and publishing contracts. They also arrange live performances and tours, and help with the general marketing of the artists. They are responsible for the general business activities and must liaise between the artists, lawyers, accountants and record/publishing company to ensure everything is going to plan. They must also motivate the artists and help direct their image. Managers are paid from an agreed percentage (generally around 20 per cent) of the artists' record, tour and promotional income. You need:

- Motivational skills
- Diplomacy
- Knowledge of how the music business works.

Tour manager

Organising the tour from putting together the tour budget to negotiating contracts with the venues and organising transport and hotels. The tour manager also hires the crew, and looks after the income and expenditure of money as well as being responsible for the artists (including dragging them out of bed in the morning) and dealing with any problems they encounter. The tour manager is responsible to the artist's management or record company to whom the accounts (which the tour manager has kept) are presented at the conclusion of the tour. You need to be:

- Logical
- Diplomatic
- Financially adept.

Booking agent

The job of the booking agent is to book their artists gigs and tours, nationally and internationally. The booker must ensure they choose the right venue for their artists – not too big and not too small, size of stage, what the acoustics are like, contract arrangements etc. – and that if playing with other artists they complement each other so the audience appreciates them. The booking agent also tries to arrange support slots with bigger bands to get them exposure. The band gets paid for each gig and the booking agent makes his/her money by taking a percentage of this. You need:

- An ability to spot potential
- A knowledge of the live music scene.

Backline technician (roadie)

The backline technicians are the men (it is rare to see women occupying this area of work) unloading and loading the vans before and after the gigs, setting up the stage equipment – the PA, monitors, instruments, microphone, manuscript and instrument stands – maintaining it while in use and very often driving the van, its equipment and passengers to their destinations. The backline technician also ensures equipment is usable and may order whatever else is necessary, e.g. guitar strings, in order to maintain the efficient delivery of the gig or tour. You need:

- To be strong enough to lift very heavy equipment
- Technical skills
- Diplomacy.

Promoter

Either the promoter or the booking agent will book the venue, depending on the level the promoter is working at. The job of the promoter is to then sell the tickets for the show/tour. This is done by advertising the performances via flyers (leaflets handed out at appropriate locations, e.g. after a show at the venue the artists are scheduled to play at), posters, radio and through relevant publications such as *NME* and *Time Out*. The promoter must make sure that the potential audience is reached to ensure sell-out performances. The promoter takes a percentage of all tickets sold. You need:

- Business skills
- Knowledge of the live music scene.

WORKING FOR A RECORD COMPANY

Label managing director

Obviously in terms of staff numbers and the specific job descriptions there are differences between major record labels and small independent labels, but basically the aim remains to sign bands, record their music and to make a profit. The majority are pop labels, making up around ten per cent of records released. The label managing director of the major companies will liaise with the different company departments such as A&R, marketing, PR, design, accounts etc., as well as artists' managers to make sure everything is going to plan and to organise new campaigns and strategies to promote different artists on their label. This involves allocating budgets. For smaller, newly formed independent labels this work may be covered by one or two people who use independent companies to help with distribution etc. Managing directors will also go to gigs to make final decisions on signing a new act and will generally motivate the company from the top. Managing directors need:

- Managerial skills
- Financial and business skills
- Experience of the music industry.

A&R (artists and repertoire)

A&R people scout for new talent to sign to their record label. They do this by listening to demo tapes sent in, by going to live shows and by listening on the musical grapevine for what is 'hot and happening'. The job involves taking risks as A&R people must sign bands that make hits so the record company can make a profit. If they sign an unsuccessful band they will ultimately lose their jobs, so decisions are never made lightly. In larger record companies the first rung of the A&R ladder is a scout, who when finding worthy talent will bring in senior A&R staff. The final decision is made by the head of A&R, or A&R manager. At first the A&R person may get the artists to demo some songs before offering a recording contract. Once a deal has been struck the A&R person will work with the artists alongside their manager and the record company organising recordings, advising on single choices, etc. You need:

- Total love and commitment to music
- Ability to spot potential.

Marketing

The people involved in marketing work closely with their artists' manager and their A&R representative to connect the artists to their potential audience in order to sell records, tickets to live performances and merchandise. This is done through a marketing campaign which can involve posters, adverts, television and radio exposure. They also get involved with making decisions on record sleeves and logos with the designers, directing the press and PR and ensuring the relevant shops are well stocked and making sales. They may also organise for their artists to sponsor brand names and for companies to sponsor their artist's tours. You need:

- Diplomacy
- Marketing skills.

Record sleeve designer

The record sleeve designers may be freelance, work for a design company or work in-house for a record label. They design the record sleeves for the artists they are working for. Initially they listen to the music and try to translate it visually. They may get input from the artists themselves and then must put down their ideas on to paper or computer and work from there, commissioning artists and photographers as necessary. You need:

- Art/design training and experience
- Ability to translate artists' music into a visual image.

Public relations

Also known as 'pluggers', people working in music PR get the artists they are working for on to radio and television, whether it be in the form of videos, live performances or interviews. Working as a plugger means you have to go out and scout for talent or you may work for a record label and would then seek publicity for the label's bands. Work involves meeting with radio and television producers and persuading them to give your artists airtime. Normally you would approach radio first, as television producers are less likely to take on anyone who hasn't already established their name on radio. You need:

- Knowledge of music and the media industry
- Perseverance.

THE RECORDING STUDIO

Studio manager

The studio manager's job is firstly to attract artists to record in the studio. This involves promoting it to record companies and meeting with A&R staff to negotiate studio prices and make deals. This also means the studio manager must keep the studio as up-to-date as necessary to avoid clients looking elsewhere. Once the artists are booked into the studio, the studio manager's job is to liaise between the different personnel involved in the recording process, i.e. producers, engineers, artists, etc. The studio manager may also have a knowledge of recording sound technology, plus:

- Sales skills
- Financial skills.

Assistant engineer and tape op

The assistant engineer assists in the studio by doing whatever is needed, from fetching sandwiches and newspapers to shifting equipment and clearing up after a session, but being available for the whole session gives the assistant the chance to learn the technicalities of recording music and how the studio works. You need:

- Technical skills
- Initiative.

Engineer

The engineer prepares the studio, setting up equipment, loading tapes etc. for the recording session. The engineer must interpret the sound requirements of the artists and producer by using the studio equipment. This may be done by mixing the tracks in a different way or using an effect to produce a different sound. The engineer will also maintain the studio equipment and make sure that any breakdowns are quickly rectified as studio time costs money. The engineer will also 'cut' the sound from the mixed tape on to the master disk from which all copies are made. The roles of the engineer may be divided up into specialist areas and may also be blurred with that of the producer. You need:

- Engineering skills
- Technical knowledge
- Diplomacy.

Producer

The producer is responsible for the overall sound of the music, not just the quality but also the feel. After deciding to work with the artists, the producer will go into preproduction with them, which is a form of rehearsal for the recording session. The recording studio is equipped with a mixing desk which – with digital technology, such as the Capricorn studio in the Penthouse at Abbey Road Studios – can have as many as 160 tracks. Each instrument and voice is recorded independently and put down on to its own track. The producer's job is to then decide whether to boost the lower and higher frequencies of each track depending on the type of sound s/he is aiming to achieve. The different tracks are then mixed together until the piece of music sounds and feels right. Producers were often previously engineers or artists. You need:

- Technical knowledge
- Tact.

OTHER AREAS OF WORK

Publishing

The publishing company works for the artists, dealing with all the administration required to collect Performing Rights Society (PRS) and Mechanical Copyright Protection Society (MCPS) money earned not just nationally but from all around the world. PRS is the money paid for broadcasting songs on television and radio or any other place where it is considered a performance, e.g. from a radio played publicly in a shop. MCPS is the percentage the songwriter/composer receives on unit record sales. Publishing companies must look for new acts to sign and work with and may be instrumental in getting them a record deal if they do not have one already. They also deal with songwriters and composers to get their work performed. The publisher will also be involved with getting music on to film and television soundtracks, and may have a specialist department for this purpose. You need:

■ Ability to recognise potential
■ Tact.

Music journalist

If you are interested in a career in music journalism just visit your local WH Smith to see the numerous publications dedicated to this subject, let alone all the newspapers which have a special music page or column. The journalist reviews performances and recordings, keeps us up to date with the latest news and carries out interviews with the performers all written in a style in keeping with the publication for which s/he is writing. The journalist is generally freelance, at least initially, but may go on to become a staff writer, which includes writing features, editing letters and reviews. Perks include being given free records, free entry to gigs and concerts to review. The journalist can move up the ranks to become a features or assistant editor and then editor. The editor is responsible for the overall style of the magazine, its contents – making sure that deadlines are kept and the text proofread etc – and making decisions on layout, design and production. You need:

■ Determination
■ Good command of language
■ Journalism skills.

Music therapist

The music therapist works with groups or individuals from children to adults for whom verbal communication is not an adequate form of self-expression, e.g. autistic children, people living with HIV/AIDS, the sensory impaired and those with psychiatric illness. By playing, singing and listening, a relationship is built up between the therapist and client. The client plays a variety of percussion and ethnic instruments in addition to their voice to develop their own 'musical language'. The therapist responds musically to support and encourage this process, with the intention of facilitating positive changes in behaviour, emotion and self-awareness. Employers include the National Health Service, local education authorities, Department of Social Services, charitable organisations and trusts. Therapists may also be self-employed. You need:

- Professional training
- Degree in music or equivalent
- Desire to help others
- Sensitivity.

Music video production

It is now a prerequisite for any pop band that a single release is accompanied by a video. It is an essential televisual promotional tool and is big business, costing on average £50,000 for a video that is likely to make it on to *Top of the Pops*. Video directors are commissioned by the record company – either from reputation or after seeing their showreels or from a number of directors pitching for the work. The director must write a financially viable treatment (written idea for the video). A producer comes on board who selects the crew and a casting director who recruits any additional extras needed. After the video is shot it is edited and delivered back to the record company, who may ask for it to be reshot or re-edited. You need:

- Video production skills
- Business skills.

Session fixer

Session fixers may be freelance or work for a company. They will be approached by a film, television, video or radio production company to find musicians to play on soundtracks, jingles or whatever music may be needed on their productions as well as to maybe write and arrange the music. Musicians are generally recruited through networking. The fixer will be allocated a budget and will find a suitable studio and musicians etc. to set up the recording session or s/he will pay for the whole process personally and charge the production company. You need:

- Experience of the recording process
- Database of session people
- Financial skills.

Music teacher

Music teachers in schools are generally classically trained and although they may teach instruments their main job is to instil into the pupils an interest and enthusiasm for music. Music teachers may also teach their specialised instrument to children in school clubs, run the school choir and organise musical performances for the parents and pupils. Teaching in schools means that you must also be a qualified teacher. Teaching outside schools includes colleges, universities, private tuition, adult education and community workshops. You need:

- Musical skills and qualifications
- Teaching qualifications
- Initiative
- Patience.

Music television presenter and VJ

Presenters and video jockeys often start out as runners (general dogsbody for a film, television or video company), researchers, journalists or come from other media-related connections. They present and interview artists and musical personalities on television, e.g. *Top of the Pops* and MTV. They may write their own material and after a rehearsal may present live to camera, which is not as easy as it looks. Their visual image and personality must also appeal to the target audience and they must not be unnerved by big celebrities. You need:

- Experience of the media industry
- 'Right' image/personality
- To be at ease in front of a camera.

Radio DJ

The DJ on the radio presents music from a list which is selected weekly by the radio producer in keeping with the style of the station, as well as playing a few independent choices. The DJ will also conduct on-air interviews with personalities, make general chat and operate the studio independently. They are responsible to the radio producer and are helped by a broadcast assistant. DJs come from a variety of backgrounds including journalism and working as a broadcast assistant. Working for hospital or community radio is a good way of getting experience. You need:

- Clear speaking voice
- Personality
- Technical skills
- Experience in some area of the media.

Club DJ

DJs are sent the most recent music releases on vinyl, which are called white labels (as that's what they have on them), from pluggers and record companies. S/he must operate the decks – which have two players for mixing between tracks so they appear seamless. The club DJ may also 'scratch' the records to produce an interesting effect. The DJ is expected to spin the 'hippest most happening grooves and tunes' to attract the punters to the club and, once there, to keep them on the dance floor for as long as possible to create an exciting atmosphere so they will want to come back. People will request tracks they want to hear and so the DJ should have a collection that can accommodate their choices. Some DJs become remixers or artists who release their own product. You need:

- Technical skill
- Knowledge of what the punters want or should want
- Extensive vinyl collection.

Distribution

Major labels have their own distribution departments, or independent companies can be used. Distributors are the people who get the CDs, vinyl and cassettes into the retail outlets around the country. The record label passes on artist news, forthcoming gigs and promotional information etc. to the distributor, who then passes it on to the retail outlets in a bid to get them to purchase some stock. Once the decision has been made by the shops to stock the record, the distributor is involved in collating and sending out the order. As distributors take a percentage of units sold they may select who and for how long they will distribute. You need:

- Understanding of the music business

- Driving licence
- Sales skills.

Merchandise

Band merchandise includes T-shirts, caps, badges and other accessories. These all have to be designed, printed and sold and that's the job of the merchandiser. The merchandiser should have an official agreement with the artists they are merchandising for, with whom they then split the profits. Percentages vary from deal to deal but usually go in the band's favour. The artists will generally help with the design to be used. Depending on the size of the merchandising company the merchandiser will get a distributor to sell their goods to the retail outlets or they'll distribute themselves. You need:

- Business skills
- Financial skills
- Knowledge of what is likely to sell
- Ability to spot potential.

Related Occupations

- Music retail
- Musical research and development
- Accountancy
- Security
- Arts administration
- Photography
- Fan club
- Libraries and archives
- Manufacturing/maintaining musical instruments
- Make-up
- Lawyer
- Caterer
- Stylist
- Community work
- Radio and television production
- Festival administrator.

CASE STUDY

Anna Maratos-Tooth, Music Therapist

Anna Maratos-Tooth qualified as a music therapist in September 1996 after completing a 12-month postgraduate course in Music Therapy at Guildhall. She now works in the psychiatric unit of a London hospital with inpatients who have severe mental illness, intensive care patients and people in the community.

How do you use music therapy?

'There is a range of ways music therapy can be used. You tend to work in a client-based way. In music therapy we aim to form a relationship via musical improvisation. The patients play percussion/ethnic instruments such as gongs, cymbals, shakers, wind chimes. Anything you can bang which will make a pleasant noise. The patients are encouraged to express themselves. I play violin or piano and we all improvise. My job is to support, direct and interact with the patients through music and depending on the level of the group various things happen. For example when working with my mentally ill inpatient group you will find they are entirely isolated in terms of interacting with one another. Normally you would all play together, but these people find it difficult to share the same speed, tempo, melody. If I try and meet them by playing at the same tempo they will immediately change it and run away. It is a cat-and-mouse situation. The aim is to create sharing and integration so that from a fragmented start you will end with a slightly more integrated finish.'

What qualifications did you need to do your postgraduate course in Music Therapy?

'You do need a degree in music, although having said that I didn't have one – my first degree is in modern languages – but I did have a very rigorous audition. I started playing the recorder at three and the cello at seven. You must be able to play the piano. That's pretty much essential, even if it is only your second instrument because it is very broad in its range. You need to have achieved at least grade 8 because it is a very fine art to be able to improvise with someone who has a mental illness without compounding the chaos.'

What advice would you give to would-be music therapists?

'Learn the piano. Get a degree in music or at least get grade 8. Go and get some experience beforehand so you understand what it is all about and don't apply too young. I think it is important to get some life experience first because it is stressful work.'

CASE STUDY

Gunilla Karlson, Junior Artist Manager for GT Management

After Gunilla Karlson graduated from Thames Valley University with a BA in Design and Media Management, she met up with a friend who told her they were looking for a personal assistant for a booking agent. It was through this contact she landed her first job.

What did your job at the booking agent entail?

'I was booking gigs for Jamiroquai before they became big. I organised big

European tours by contacting promoters and venues with the right capacity, etc. It was good because I got to go to all these gigs for free. I got the PA job because music people like to take on people they know. The whole company folded after a while because Jamiroquai left.'

What did you do then?

'I put a notice up in the Camalot Centre on the Kensal Road in Ladbroke Grove where there are studios and a bar etc., saying I was available to work on anything to do with the media. I was contacted by this lady who was making a feature film and was recruited as the music supervisor on the strength that I had experience of working in the music business. This was a voluntary position and involved me putting the sound track together by finding music that went with the nature of the film. I then had to clear the music by getting rights for as little money as possible. One of the songs I needed was by Chezere and that's how I met Guy (from Head On Management). Then it transpired the film was never going to make it and Guy's PA was leaving, so he gave me the job.'

What does your current job entail?

'If anyone wants to get to the artist they have to come through me. I am the scapegoat between the profession/public and the artist. I am in daily communication with artists, publishers, record companies – trying to get publishing and recording contracts, speaking with lawyers, arranging tours etc., trying to get money for our artists from record companies, tour supports. There are two types of support, one where the fees cover the expenses and there is a shortfall and the record company covers the shortfall, or the record company pays for your artist to do a support.'

What advice would you give to people wanting to break into the industry?

'Go to nightclubs and meet the right people and blag backstage. Sell yourself for a year for very little money as a work placement, receptionist, slave. This will give you an overview of how the industry works and you will make those first initial contacts. Then use your contacts or Handles [employment agency], or temping, to work your way in and always appear enthusiastic.'

Chapter 2
DRAMA

'When I got into drama school I thought, "I've done it!" but I hadn't. Then my third year neurosis was getting an agent and when I had got one I thought, "I've done it!", but I hadn't. Then I thought, I've got to get work. When I got my first work I thought, "I've done it!", but I hadn't. It just doesn't work like that in acting. You don't just start on one rung of the ladder and go up each step. You can get work and then not get any more for a long while or you cannot get any work for years and suddenly start getting really good work. In acting there is no rhyme or reason, no career curve. You can go up and down all the time or simply just stay on the same level.' *Gabriella Meara, Actor, Central School of Speech and Drama*

Competition

There are approximately 36,000 members of Equity – the trade union representing performers in arts and entertainment (see Directory) – and an average member is expected to work for about 12.4 weeks of the year. However, the actual number of weeks worked annually is probably higher than this figure as the sample used for this statistic included around 25 per cent of members who are no longer active in the entertainment industry. However, only a small minority of Equity members have regular jobs, with notable exceptions such as TV soap opera casts and members of standing ballet and opera companies.

The drama industry is very competitive and work insecure, which is why many actors will have to find jobs as waiters and bar staff. They have to make up their income somehow, but to be available at short notice for castings, auditions and work means they have to choose employment that gives them the flexibility and time off to do this. It is rarely possible for young people intent on becoming professional actors to find a secondary career that is personally fulfilling.

31

'Resting'?

A wide cross-section of personalities is attracted to acting or the drama industry, but let's make one thing clear. It's not glamorous, spending the majority of the year 'resting' – the actor's term for being out of work. Actors constantly attend castings and auditions for which you must be prepared to receive criticism (not always constructive) and rejection. It is also not going to make you fantastically rich, unless you are a big name in the West End theatres, film and/or television. Not only is pay rather low, but the hours are long, and because of your commitment to daily rehearsals and then evening productions you will have very little social life outside of your theatrical circle. If you want to go into drama you have to be fully dedicated and love what you do. If your intentions are not completely and utterly serious then don't bother. You will face too many rejections to survive.

Actors

Not all actors, directors and theatrical staff go through a course of training, but it is a distinct advantage as it shows you have reached a certain standard, particularly if the drama school has a good reputation with the industry. Getting into drama school is not easy as there are few places to meet the demand of the would-be professional. It is worth getting as much experience as you can before you apply by performing or getting involved in school and college plays. Joining an amateur dramatic group is also a good way to get started in drama and get some experience. The National Association of Youth Theatres has a database of around 500 active youth theatre groups around the country. For some groups, entry is by audition but generally this is not necessary, although in many cases there is a waiting list because of the numbers of people wanting to join.

Go to theatre tours to see behind the scenes and get a glimpse of what theatre life is like, e.g. The Royal National Theatre, and for those who wish to pursue a career in film, either in front of or behind the camera, why not contact the National Film and Television School or a similar institute in your area and find out if they need any help in making their student productions? Helping out on a student production will give you good experience as well as an addition for your CV, demonstrating your commitment to your chosen career to a potential employer.

Additional talents

An additional talent, such as horse-riding, playing the violin or dancing, may also help you get work.

Market yourself

The main thing to remember about the drama industry is that it is a business, not just a craft, and ultimately you have to do both if you want to succeed. This means you have to know how to market yourself as well as your talent.

ATTRIBUTES

Look at the personal attributes and skills below to see if you've got what it takes to work in the drama industry:

- Luck
- Determination
- Dedication
- Confidence
- Tenacity
- Enthusiasm
- Good communication skills
- Ability to work well in a team
- Ability to market yourself
- Ability to accept criticism and rejection
- Knowledge of the drama industry.

There is no particular personality required to be an actor. Training and gaining qualifications are helpful to working in theatre and other relevant media, but getting experience (paid or unpaid) is all-important to demonstrate your commitment to your chosen career.

CASE STUDY

Stewart Wright, Actor – credits include the leading role in BBC1 series, *Rescue Me* with Sally Phillips and *Wild West* with Dawn French

How did you get into acting?

'I did some child acting when I was about seven. Someone who was working in advertising saw me being overexcited at a kids' party and suggested I got an agent. I did some adverts and radio, and my agent wanted me to go the States to work or to go to stage school. My mum did not think that was a good idea and wanted me to get a proper education instead. I did lots of acting at school, directing myself in plays. By about 15 or 16 I was set on becoming an actor. My parents were not into the idea at all. I pacified them by saying I would go to three auditions for drama schools and if I didn't get in, I would give up the idea and get a proper job or do some other kind of training. I didn't get into the first two drama schools, but I got into the third. I did my BA in Acting at the Central School of Speech and Drama from 1993 to 1996. We did lots of showcases in the last year that were open to the business and public. I had a few agents interested in me, but I had to do all the leg-work and badger someone to act as my agent.'

What did you get out of your time at drama school, and what were the drawbacks?

'It gives you an understanding of dialogues used by directors, and their different styles – nothing can faze you. What's not good about drama school is that it is so singly focused. All you do is acting with other actors – there is no life outside, no balance. It's not like at university where you do other things like sports. Acting is literally all you do. It's very insular.'

How did you get your first break?

'I was working as a line reader, reading lines for other actors in auditions – a job I got through my drama school. The assistant who was working there left after three months to cast comedy at the BBC, and she got me my first proper part in *People Like Us*. I then went on to do the TV comedy circuit, sitcoms and sketch shows. It progressed to drama roles and theatre until my leading role in the BBC1 series, *Rescue Me*. I am now working with Dawn French on a comedy series called *Wild West* which is due to be screened in the autumn (2002).'

What are the pros and cons of working in acting?

'It is a very difficult lifestyle for other people around you to live in if they don't have an understanding of the industry. It is a very unstructured life to cope with. You also have to be able to cope with rejection, competitiveness and how deep you have to dig when it is not happening for you. The positive side is that I love acting and it is really exciting when you work. You have the opportunity to touch people – make them laugh or make them think – and that is really rewarding.'

What advice would you give to aspiring young actors?

'I remember asking exactly the same question to Robert Hardy (from *All Creatures Great and Small*) when I was at school. He replied that the best advice is, "don't!"

Which is what I would say. I guess anyone who really wants to be an actor will disregard my advice, but it will filter out the ones who aren't *really* serious. Only become an actor if that's all you want to do – if it is the purpose that you are here for . . . otherwise find a much happier life somewhere else.'

CASE STUDY

Caroline Giles, Make-up Artist/Designer, Yorkshire Television

Caroline Giles did a City and Guilds course in Hairdressing, which together with her art portfolio gained her entry onto the BTEC HND in Theatrical Studies (now a degree course) at the London College of Fashion. Since completing her studies, Caroline has worked in both television and theatre and is now a staff member at Yorkshire Television (YTV).

What work have you done since graduating?

'I first went to Hong Kong to see a friend, taking my portfolio with me, and then called every single film company I found in the phone book. I subsequently met a few people and did a little bit of photographic make-up. From one of these sessions I got to work on *Soldier Soldier* – the television series. I was paid a fairly good salary for a trainee – £380 a week.

'When I returned to the UK I met my wig dressing teacher from the London College of Fashion who told me about *My Fair Lady* doing a theatre tour. I sent my CV and which Louise, the wig mistress, liked as it was well presented and showed I had some experience as well as being recommended and I was put on trial for three weeks. I ended up doing the whole seven-month tour. We were given £85 a week subsistence on top of wages to pay for accommodation.

'When I returned from tour I immediately sent off my CV to make-up designers and production companies keeping a huge file together containing information on when I sent letters, who to and their responses. I had reams and reams of letters in that file. I sent my CV to wig departments and theatrical companies and then I got a phone call from a wig master whose assistant was leaving and needed a replacement for the last week of Eliza Dolittle in the West End. This led to further theatrical work. I then went on to work as a make-up trainee on the BBC's *All Quiet on the Preston Front* and another West End production, *City of Angels*, when I was told they were looking for a trainee at YTV. I faxed my CV and had two interviews and a make-up test. I had to make one side of a lady's face up very naturally and the other side I had to age her and use a hair piece to create a 60s hair style.'

What's your job title and description?

'There are different grades within the make-up department. When I work on

Emmerdale I am the make-up designer. I have to get up very early, read the scripts and do a breakdown to ensure the continuity of each character – what they do in each story – note injuries, weddings or anything different that happens. If you are the designer you have to discuss with the director to make sure they get what they want and go through the call sheet. I have one assistant although we get in extras if they are required on the days. These would be from YTV or freelancers.'

What's the difference between theatre and television?

'In the theatre you are doing the same thing every day, whereas in TV there is a constant variety. No two days are the same. You must always think ahead to what you will need. It can be very boring, hanging around, but it is a very social job. You do a lot of talking and chatting on set, especially when you are working on something like *Emmerdale* where you get to work with the same people. If you are a freelancer you might not know the crew at all.'

THE JOBS

The personal attributes and skills listed under each job description are in addition to the ones highlighted in the previous section.

Actor

An actor must take on a character devised by a writer and convey this to the audience by using his/her body and voice under the supervision of a director. There are various avenues open to actors – West End, fringe and pub theatre, television, radio, film, commercials, voice-overs, video/computers and corporate/educational films, but securing work for any of them is not easy, particularly if you haven't got an agent. Although being a member of Equity is no longer essential to secure work on television and film etc., Equity status is still regarded by some as a mark of quality and many prefer to use Equity members above non-Equity members. Acting contracts are often short-term and not particularly well-paid unless you are a well-known film star such as Samuel L Jackson or Nicole Kidman. Actors may specialise in a particular genre, such as theatre or comedy, and may have to learn scripts overnight. The majority will have trained in drama. All actors must be prepared to face rejection and to find alternative work while 'resting'. You need:

- Talent – empathy and imagination
- Stamina
- Good memory
- Self-discipline
- Ambition.

Production manager/administrator/executive director

The production manager is the person with the overall managerial and financial responsibility. The production manager will be the one to select the play and recruit the director. If the production manager is not already connected to a production house (i.e. his/her own theatre) s/he will also find the theatre to rent and raise all the necessary capital to put on the play. This is raised from a number of different independent sources such as writers and business people and also from arts organisations. S/he will be responsible for paying the staff and other necessary expenditure. The production manager will coordinate all the different department activities to ensure they are keeping within budget and to deadline. It will also be up to the production manager to decide how long the play should run and to close it down if not making the required revenue. You need:

- Diplomacy
- Managerial skills
- Persuasiveness
- Theatrical experience.

Director

The director is the person responsible for interpreting the script into the live play. It is the director's vision which, while liaising with the set designer, lighting designer and costume designer, will be translated within budget. The director also casts or helps to cast the actors for the play and then directs their characters' roles during rehearsals. The director also coordinates all the backstage and technical crew and keeps everyone motivated. Directors usually come from an acting or stage management background, or may have trained in directing at drama school or university and worked their way up from an assistant or trainee director. You need:

- Assertiveness
- Creativity
- Persuasiveness
- Experience of theatre.

Casting director

The casting director is the person who casts the different actors for the play. Final decisions may need to be verified by the director and possibly the production manager, but the casting director is the person who finds the actors from whom to select. Casting directors visit drama schools and fringe productions to find suitable actors as well as through acting agencies. Casting directors will only be found working with large theatrical companies or for television and film. The director will do the castings for smaller companies. The casting director will arrange for the actors to come and audition for the various parts and will negotiate their contracts with their agents. You need:

- Diplomacy
- Ability to spot new talent
- Vision.

DESIGN

Set designer

The set designer, together with the ideas laid out by the director, will interpret the script and draw sketches of the floor plan and/or make a smaller scale model of the stage as the designer sees it. Once these designs have been agreed, technical drawings giving detailed measurements and materials to be used are made up. Depending on the size of the company the set will be built by professional set builders, or for smaller companies the set designer may get involved. The set designer, together with the stage manager, will also be responsible for drawing up a list of props which will then have to be made or found. When the set is finally constructed, technical rehearsals will take place when the set designer can deal with any problems that might be encountered, such as a door jamming or additional props needed. The set designer may also design the costumes in smaller companies – see below. The set designer must keep within budget. You need:

- Design skills and qualifications
- Theatrical experience
- Research skills
- Good visual skills
- Creativity.

Costume designer

The costume designer is responsible for designing the costumes to be worn by the actors in the play. S/he will work alongside the director to translate the script visually in terms of what clothes should be worn. This can be anything from period costumes to a dragon's suit and will require research and inspiration. The costume designer must consider whether there will be a need for quick costume changes and how best the actor can be aided by the design of the costume. The costume designer will then sketch the costumes from which the costume makers will work. The costume designer will also supervise the making of the costumes, hire costumes, find accessories, attend the fittings to ensure the garments fit the actors and be available at the dress rehearsal to make any adjustments as necessary. The costume designer also often designs the set – see above. You need:

- Design skills and qualifications
- Good visual skills
- Creativity
- Research skills.

Stage/theatre technicians

Technicians include those responsible for lighting and sound, as well as the crew who move and change the scenes during performances and operate the curtains. These are the people who invariably dress in black and appear on the stage when the lights go down, so when the lights come back on, the scene has miraculously changed from a cosy living room to a country garden. Sets are often very heavy and the technicians must be able to shift them very quickly so that the audience hardly has time to notice anything has happened. You need:

- Physical strength
- Speed.

Lighting

In large companies a lighting designer will be in charge of a team of electricians, but in smaller companies will operate the whole lighting system personally. Lighting is used not just to illuminate the play, but to create colour, special effects and mood. The lighting designer will go over the script with the director to discuss what is required. The lighting designer will also liaise with the set designer, costume designer, make-up designer and stage management and will then draw up a lighting plan. The lights will then be rigged up by the team if there is one, or the lighting designer, who will then operate the lighting system. Some lighting designers use computers both to draw up the lighting plan and to operate the lighting in the production. The technical rehearsal will show up any problems that might arise and it is the responsibility of the lighting designer to then rectify them. You need:

- Good visual sense
- Creativity
- Electrical knowledge
- Lighting skills.

Sound

The work of the sound designer is to produce voice amplification and create sound effects (e.g. a bird singing or a thunderbolt) as needed in the play. The sound designer will go through the script with the director and discuss sound effects needed. Any sound effects the sound designer will not be creating personally will have to be found from other sources such as a sound effects library. The sound designer will be responsible for the voice amplification and sound effects during the performances, if these are not being operated by an electrician. You need:

- Technical skills
- Recording skills
- Creativity.

Stage manager

The stage manager must organise the smooth running of rehearsals, making sure the actors are present when required and that timetables are adhered to. The stage manager also ensures that the technicians are aware of any changes which occur to the script, and that costumes are made, props found and sets constructed to deadline. The stage manager makes notes regarding scene changes, sound effects, lighting, actors' cues and so on, in order that s/he can advise the technicians of when they must go into action. In very large theatres, the stage manager may give out directions to the stage technicians via headsets. An assistant stage manager may assist by prompting actors during rehearsals and 'on the night' and will ensure the props are ready for use. They may also call actors during performances (when it's time to go on stage). You need:

■ To be responsible
■ Managerial skills
■ A good memory.

Production staff

Production staff are the personnel who construct the sets and props for a production. In large companies the production staff will have several different departments specialising in different areas of the production process: these include carpentry, scenic painting, metalwork, armoury and props. For smaller companies, the props and the armoury may be hired and the carpentry work commissioned from an external source. They are all ultimately responsible to the set designer who will oversee the whole production process. The production staff will also be responsible for dealing with repairs to the set should they be needed. After the production is finished the sets and props must be looked after and kept in the theatre store. You need:

■ Attention to detail
■ Specialist craft skills
■ Design skills
■ Historical knowledge.

Wardrobe

The wardrobe department must translate the costume designer's ideas into garments within budget and to deadline. This requires drawing up patterns, purchasing appropriate fabrics – which may then need dyeing – and of course making up the garment. Appropriate clothes may also be hired or purchased from specialist stores or markets. Research needs to be conducted to ensure the details of the costume are correct. Costumes must be fitted to ensure they are the right size for the actor. The wardrobe department must also repair or alter any costumes as necessary – as well as clean and iron them – and store them between performances. They may also help to dress the actors prior to the performance and during quick costume changes. The wardrobe department will also be responsible for making or finding shoes, hats and other accessories which may be required. You need:

- Ability to make up patterns
- Sewing skills
- Attention to detail
- Creativity.

Wigs and make-up

Most actors in the theatre will apply their own make-up, which is something they will have learnt to do at drama school. Theatrical make-up is over emphasised so the audience may see actors' features more clearly from a distance. Make-up departments do exist in some cases, particularly if more intricate make-up details, such as prosthetics, are required, and in television where cameras allow us to view the actors' faces close-up. Wigmaking, which includes facial hair, is a specialist art and will be undertaken by the make-up personnel. The make-up department will be responsible for any touching up or refitting of wigs required during performances. You need:

- Make-up skills/training
- Hairdressing skills/training
- Creativity
- Tact.

House manager

The house manager is responsible for the organised running of the theatre. S/he hires the staff to sell and collect tickets, run the bar or cafe, make the building secure and do the cleaning within budget. The house manager will deal with any problems brought up by the audience such as double booking of seats. You need:

- Managerial skills
- Experience of the theatre.

Box office

The main concern of box office staff is to sell tickets. This can be done in person, via telephone and post or through an agent. For small studio theatres seats are non-reserved so people can sit where they like. In larger theatres seats are allocated with a letter and a number to show their position in the theatre. Prices vary according to seat position. Box office staff must cross seats off on their seating plan as tickets are sold. This is now normally done on computer, which makes the system efficient and simple to use. It will also show you very quickly how many seats are still available. The box office staff, particularly in smaller theatres, may also be involved with the marketing and promotional functions of the theatre as well as keeping accounts. They deal with the general public, giving information and advice on current and forthcoming performances. You need:

- Marketing skills
- Financial skills.

Marketing and promotions/press office

Attracting an audience to the show – within budget – is the responsibility of the marketing and promotions department. The marketing and promotions personnel write press releases about the play to send to the local and (if applicable) national press. Local radio and television may also be targeted. They will also set up interviews with the actors or director and the media.

Complimentary tickets are always sent out to the media to encourage them to attend and review the play. Freelance photographers are generally commissioned to take the photos to send to the press and for adverts, posters and front of house displays as well as for use in the programmes. The marketing and promotions staff will also produce the programme, which, depending on the size of the company, may be very extensive, containing a cast list, cast biographies, photographs, reviews, background to the play and its history and advertisements. They will also produce information leaflets on future productions. You need:

- Marketing skills
- Creativity.

Dramatherapy

The drama therapist works with groups or individuals from children to adults. The aim is to try and build some form of relationship with their clients through the medium of drama using techniques such as improvisation and mime. Their clients do not generally find verbal communication an adequate form of self-expression. Clients include those with a physical or learning disability or psychiatric illness. Drama therapists are professionals who come from a drama, health, social or educational background. You need:

- Professional training
- Maturity
- Desire to help others
- Sensitivity.

Agent

Agents are managers who find work for their clients in theatre, film, television, radio, commercials, corporate videos and for personal performances. Their client list may be specialist but can include actors, some technicians, comedians, musicians and performers. They recruit people on to their books by visiting drama schools, recommendations, going to see plays, and by artists contacting them. They take on a new client who has outstanding talent or if they have a special attribute or skill which may come in useful, e.g. can ride a horse. They find work for their clients by talking to people involved in casting for productions to find out what sort of person they are looking for. They will then send to them their client's photograph and information on their previous experience. The actor will then go for an audition or interview. When the agent secures work for their clients they will take a percentage of the payment, which varies according to the medium they will be working in. The agent also has to counsel his/her clients when they face rejection. You need:

- Managerial skills
- Persuasiveness
- Knowledge of the media and theatrical industries
- Tact
- Ability to spot potential.

Drama teacher

Teaching people of all ages, not simply to act, but to gain spatial awareness, free up their imagination and generally become more self-confident, is the role of the drama teacher. In schools, teaching means you must also be a qualified teacher. You will be responsible for staging the school's theatrical productions and organising theatre trips to see plays and backstage. Teaching outside schools includes colleges, universities, adult education, amateur dramatic companies and theatrical clubs. You need:

- Dramatic/acting skills
- Teaching qualifications
- Initiative
- Patience
- Creativity.

Related Occupations

- Theatrical support organisations
- Script writing
- Bar staff and catering in theatres
- Photography
- Dance (see below)
- Merchandise
- Theatre research
- Role play workshops for business, prisons and health centres
- Working for the Arts Council
- Booking agencies

- Ushers and programme selling
- Arts and community associations
- Music (see above)
- Speech therapy
- Public relations.

CASE STUDY

Marc Wootton, Trainee Director, Orange Tree Theatre

After doing A-levels in Theatre Studies, Psychology and Literature, Marc Wooton went on to obtain a First Class Honours degree in Drama at Exeter University. He is now a trainee director at the Orange Tree Theatre in Richmond. The traineeship involves learning about directing through observation and direct involvement in rehearsals. He also acts as assistant director for the main house shows. This involves doing anything from making tea for the actors, to directing if the director is unavailable. Marc also learns about administration and the general running of the theatre which includes front-of-house, box office and artistic decisions. His year attachment gives him the opportunity to form relationships with all the departments, and allows him to direct two plays, *The Stringless Marion-ette* and *The Second Cosmic Hair Gallery*.

How did you come to work at the Orange Tree Theatre?

'While I was at university and after I graduated I wrote to loads of places. I had worked for two weeks voluntarily with Patrick Sandford at the Nuffield Theatre, so I had some work experience. I must have written about 200 letters, to every theatre in England. I had some photocopied letters saying they'd keep my name on file and a few letters offering personal advice, including one from Alan Ayckbourn. I then did a stage management job with the Battersea Arts Centre which I got through a contact at the Young Vic. I subsequently joined a theatre company down in Exeter and went on tour to France. When I returned I received a letter from the Orange Tree saying they were looking for a trainee director and would like to meet me. I had an interview, and was recalled and selected. They have two trainee posts every year, one starts in September and the other in August. I didn't have to do any directing at the interviews, but my references were important.'

What advice do you have for people interested in going into theatre?

'You can do a course in a specific area or get a wider education, which I believe is better as it leaves your options open and there aren't that many jobs out there so you need to be realistic. Get in contact with a local theatre or arts centre. Just help out and get some work experience. Find out why you like theatre. Ask to sell programmes, paint the set, help behind the bar or be a general dogsbody. Get in on a voluntary basis because being there is the best way to find out which job interests you most.'

CASE STUDY

Karen Adams, Marketing and Press Manager, Orange Tree Theatre

During Karen's last year at university, where she studied for a BA in English and Sociology, she undertook some voluntary work for the Nuffield Theatre in Southampton. She worked for the press department for one day a week for a year. After graduating, the person she had been assisting at the theatre left and she was offered the job from 20 other interviewees. 'The post was considered a trainee position but did require the applicant to have some experience and I had gained that through my voluntary work where I started writing press releases, etc.'

Karen now works at the Orange Tree Theatre in Richmond as the marketing and press manager. Her work involves putting together press releases, designing brochures, getting advertising space and allocation of budget. The post was advertised in the *Guardian* and Karen had to send in her CV and go through two rounds of interviews. She was selected from ten interviewees.

What qualifications, skills and attributes do you need to work in theatre?

'Do some voluntary work and learn on the job, mock up a press release – remember every theatre has their own house style. Most posts will require you to have a degree but it doesn't seem to matter too much what it's in. Be persistent – there are very few jobs around so you do have to keep pushing and get along with everyone, including the press.'

What productions have you worked on?

'I have worked on everything from Shakespeare's *Macbeth* to new musicals – a wide variety because I have always worked at producing theatres.'

Any advice?

'Get some voluntary experience as you are highly unlikely to be employed without it, and get as much out of that as you can. Be really persistent if you have a lead or know of a job coming up.'

achieve your ambitions

world leading dance facilities

unrivalled dance artist training at
undergraduate and graduate level

Performance   Choreography
Repertory   Technique
Scenography   Dance Science
Community Dance Research

LABAN

LABAN CREEKSIDE   T: +44 (0)20 8691 8600
LONDON SE8 3DZ   F: +44 (0)20 8691 8400
E: INFO@LABAN.ORG   WWW.LABAN.ORG

Chapter 3
DANCE

London is the key area for dance, with at least 150 dance companies and 80 per cent of dance artists based in the capital. There are, however, well developed scenes in other areas of the UK, particularly the north of England and Scotland. There has been a growing trend towards community dance too, with nearly five million people each week involved in community dance in the UK.

London Arts is currently reviewing the infrastructure for independent dance managers in the capital. The review will provide several outcomes, including an improved working life for independent dance artists, audiences and managers, and recommendations for funding.

Competition

Although not quite as fierce as for musicians and actors, finding work for the professional dancer is an extremely competitive business. Most people who have chosen dance as their vocation will have begun dance classes in childhood, and those wishing to pursue a career in ballet would have commenced training at least by their early teenage years. An early start is necessary to build up the strength, muscle tone, flexibility and stamina required for the rigorous schedule of the professional dancer. Dancing, or training to dance, for a living is extremely hard work, and daily practice and evening performances are not for the faint- or half-hearted. Training or professional, it's a seven-day week.

Professional training

Professional training starts from the age of 16, although younger people will be involved in weekend and evening classes if they don't already go to a specialist school. Total commitment to dancing is necessary, as is a professional training course if you want to follow a dancing career. Getting on to a professional dancing course, however, is not easy as places are highly sought after.

Short careers

There are three main categories of dance style; ballet, contemporary and non-western, but all dancers, whatever their style, tend to be self-employed or freelance with little job security. Added to this the pay is not high for new entrants. You can also expect a short performing career. It is unlikely you will dance beyond your mid-thirties – and serious injury can shorten a dancer's career still earlier – so it is necessary to think about the direction your career will move in after your performance career is ended.

> 'The most common reason for leaving a ballet career is back injuries in men and hips in women. We have an osteopath for remedial care, a sports psychologist and nutritionist because you can cause injuries through bad diet and negative thinking. We also have a physiotherapist to help us relax more. The general aches and pains we get tend to be overcome during the morning class.' *Toby Smith, Ballet Dancer and Student*

Dance UK is currently undertaking a second survey of dancers' health and injury in the UK. The first report lead to the Dance UK's Healthier Dancer Programme and a special insurance scheme for dancers by Equity. The 2002 survey will look at the existing health of dancers, what causes the injury, the financial consequence and issues to consider for the future.

What next?

Some dancers do go on to do choreography, teaching or fulfil the more administrative roles within dance companies and organisations. In recent times the dance profession has grown, which has opened up new career options. Dance movement therapy and raising the profile of dance within the community as a dance animateur (see page 56) are examples. Most performers leave the dance industry altogether as all jobs are heavily oversubscribed.

Of course you may not be entering the dance industry as a performer, wanting to follow a related career path, but most who choose this route will have had some dance training – maybe of a non-professional nature – or relevant experience. Go to see as many different genres of dance as you can. The two biggest dance festivals in England are Spring Loaded (organised by The Place Theatre and the South Bank Centre) from February to May, and the Dance Umbrella (programmed by the British Umbrella) in the autumn. Get to know the important people within the industry, read whatever you can on the subject and get the necessary training. In any case a knowledge of the industry together with some training is vital in securing employment.

ATTRIBUTES

You will require certain attributes to be part of the dance industry. Do the attributes listed below apply to you?

- Talent
- Technique
- Appreciation of music
- Ability to understand and portray a character
- Good general health
- Physical fitness
- Stamina
- Ability to accept rejection/criticism
- Flexibility
- Dedication
- Ability to work well in a team.

For those not pursuing a performance career, knowledge and experience (paid or voluntary) is essential to getting in to the industry. For the professional dancer, training is essential, you won't become one without it, as is a total love of and commitment to dance to pull you through the hard times and help you progress in your chosen career.

CASE STUDY

Della, Professional Dancer and Dance Teacher

Della has been in the dance business since she was eight. She started off with the London City Ballet Company who performed at many top London theatres including Sadler's Wells and in front of the late Diana, Princess of Wales. Since completing her full-time training at Performers' Dance College she has worked consistently, starting with summer seasons, cruises and panto. Della is now fulfilling one of her dreams by dancing professionally for many top selling recording artists, including Kylie Minogue, S Club, Spice Girls, Steps and Robbie Williams. She also teaches tap and jazz to children.

What made you become interested in dance?

'Originally it started off as a hobby that my mother put me in to prevent me from watching too much TV as a child and it gradually progressed from there. From one class a week to dancing every night after school.'

Where did you train?

'My first school was Laine Theatre Arts, which I attended part-time from the age of eight, until I was 12. I then went to Alexandra Barnes' School of Dancing, who was my ballet teacher at Laine's, until I was 16. Finally, I went to Performers Dance College for three years where I studied ballet, tap, jazz, modern, *pas de deux*, drama, contemporary and singing full-time.'

What criteria did you need to fulfil to pass the audition?

'The audition for performers started with a ballet class taken by Susan Stephen (one of the directors of the college) then a jazz class taken by Brian Rogers (the other director) and then individually we had to perform our own piece which was choreographed by myself to a piece of music cut to one and a half minutes. We then had an interview with the directors.'

Did you work at all whilst training?

'I had no part-time job as such, but we did do shows for Brian Rogers which we were paid for.'

Do you belong to any unions or organisations?

'When I first left college I had my provisional Equity card. Within a year of leaving I gained my full membership – but I no longer pay my subscription as Equity doesn't seem to have any power within the industry. Compared to the Musicians' Union, Equity pales into insignificance. I do believe there should be a separate organisation for dancers.'

What are the pros and cons of working in dance and what advice would you give to someone seeking to work in this field?

'No day is ever the same. You are constantly meeting new people. You can be treated like royalty one day, then be expected to change in the toilets the next. Dancers suffer a lot of stereotyping and we are treated in accordance with our clients' perception of dancers. You need to be confident and to believe in yourself, especially when people are constantly knocking you back. You need to be confident with your image and be able to follow the trend and adapt it to suit you. In the commercial world your look/image is just as important, if not more important, as how well you dance. Who you know is always a great help too. It also helps to have someone you can really trust – a lot of friends and family will say what they think you want to hear which doesn't bode well in this business – your friends and family will always think you are great, but casting directors will say what they see which might not always be nice or what you want to hear. The business gets younger and younger every year, so the later you start the harder it gets.'

The Biz

Sara Matthews, Assistant Director, Central School of Ballet

Sara Matthews is the assistant director at the Central School of Ballet where she oversees the artistic content of the dance course at the school and looks after the students as well as teaching classical ballet, contemporary dance and choreography.

What is the yearly intake at Central School of Ballet?

'For our professional course it's 30 a year, but always significantly fewer boys than girls. I suppose it is not traditional for boys to go to ballet as it is for girls, therefore fewer boys present for audition at 16. The professional training course is three years and the main focus is classical ballet which includes pointework, pas de deux, allegro character and repertoire classes. Our students also study contemporary dance to a high level and cover music, jazz, singing and A-levels. The students have to be at least 16 and we would not normally take in anyone over the age of 20 – this is because it is a very short career and also the physique needs to be malleable in order to be trained properly.'

How do you assess the candidates who apply to Central School of Ballet?

'Initially they have to send us their application form and photos and references from their current academic school and dance school. They then have an audition which is a classical class and a small amount of contemporary dance to see how they can move. They also have an orthopaedic exam and spend a day at the school. They then have an interview and a final audition which also assesses their musical potential.'

Do students drop out and why?

'One or two students might leave within a couple of months of starting the course. This is more from shock when they realise how physically demanding the day is – they spend about six hours a day dancing – so they find out pretty quickly. This doesn't happen too often as the selection process is supposed to ensure that we get the right kind of student. The other kind of problems are physical – which don't show up in the orthopaedic exam. Injuries which force a student to leave occur very rarely. Another way might be if the student doesn't develop in a way that technically they need to be in order to be a professional standard at the end of the course, and we would therefore help them to discover a more appropriate direction to work towards, be that a university degree or whatever.'

What advice would you give to those seeking a dancing career?

'As in any profession there are good teachers and bad teachers. Go and look at all the schools in your area and chose the one with the best students. Be prepared for a lot of hard work and don't start dancing later than ten or 11. It is a great thing for kids to do. It gives them physical awareness, coordination and musicality. There are dancers who start at 14 or 16 but they are the exception to the rule. This is even true of contemporary dance. There are some forms of dance which you can't really learn until you have the intellectual maturity to learn or study them, but even so you really need to discover about yourself physically and also to develop muscle tone and flexible joints for dancing at an early age.'

THE JOBS

The personal attributes and skills listed under each job description are in addition to those highlighted in the previous section.

Performer

The dance performer, accompanied by music, uses the movement of his/her body to communicate with the audience. There are many genres of dance which include classical ballet, contemporary (freer and more informal kind of dance) and non-western dance (such as flamenco and salsa). Other forms of dance include jazz, tap, acrobatics and disco. These kinds of dancers are more likely to perform in musicals or cabaret including some broadcast work. As well as performing in theatres, dancers work in film and television, Christmas pantomimes, and other public places such as restaurants, art centres and schools. Once the dancer joins a company s/he may also be involved with initiating ideas for the dance piece and giving workshops with the rest of the dance company to a wide variety of people within the community and beyond. Dancers, ballet in particular, are unlikely to be dancing professionally after their mid-thirties. You need:

- Good memory
- Creativity

- Versatility
- Dance training and experience.

Teacher

Dance teachers can work full- or part-time, teaching children, adults or both. Teachers usually have greater opportunities for employment than performers and can teach in primary and secondary school where dance has now become part of the National Curriculum (physical education) in state education. Dance teachers are also required in universities and colleges and there are opportunities for teachers of recreational and vocational dance outside of the state sector in dance schools, studios, adult education institutes and community centres where they may teach individuals or groups. Dance teachers may not have to have formal qualifications to teach dance in the private sector but will have achieved a high level of dance training with relevant dance qualifications. In state schools, teachers will be professionally qualified. Contact the International Dance Teachers' Association (see Directory). You need:

- High level of dance training
- Patience
- Good communication skills
- Teaching qualifications
- Creativity
- Ability to motivate and encourage.

Choreographer

A choreographer conceives and arranges the dance piece. In order to do this the choreographer must have a good knowledge of dance and the body, combined with a strong imagination. Choreographers are usually experienced former dancers although they may also be active performers. Choreography is often a route performers take once their dancing career is coming to an end, but it is possible to start your career as a choreographer once you have completed specialist training. Choreographers may lead dance companies or be employed to work in opera or for a pop band such as S Club. You need:

- Inventiveness
- Originality
- Vision
- Practical dance experience
- Good communication skills.

Dance journalist/publishing

Working in dance journalism and publishing is probably undertaken by people who were formerly dancers as it is necessary to have a good knowledge of dance, and practical experience is extremely useful. Dance journalists attend a lot of dance performances which they then review for the dance press or special section of a local or national paper. The work is not well paid and writers normally supplement their income in various other ways, e.g. choreography and/or teaching. There are not many writers as opportunities for freelance work is not common. It is useful to have had some journalism training. You need:

- Experience and knowledge of dance
- Journalism training
- Good writing skills
- Good communication skills.

Dance animateur

Dance animateurs are community dance workers who work within a specific geographical area to raise the profile, access, participation and quality of dance in that area, funded by the Arts Councils and local authorities. Dance animateurs work with a variety of groups of all ages from children and young adults to senior citizens. They may work with those who are pursuing a dancing career or who need dance for recreation and expression, including disabled people or those in hospitals and prisons. You need:

- Relevant dance qualifications
- Administrative and organisational skills
- Driving licence
- Initiative.

Dance movement therapy

The dance movement therapist works with individuals and groups, using movement in a creative way to build a relationship between the therapist and the people s/he is working with when verbal communication is not appropriate. The therapist creates a safe environment in which the participants' movements can be explored and recognised. You need:

■ Knowledge
■ Maturity
■ Relevant professional skill and training.

Visual design for dance

Designing for dance involves transforming the dance ideas into a visual presentation, which includes using specialist lighting techniques. The lighting rig for a dance performance is quite different from that for a concert or theatre. In dance a lot of side light is used to make sure the whole body is defined, as well as light from the cyclorama – back sheet. In theatre a lot of lighting is used from the front of the stage but this is not the case in dance. The designer will experiment with sound and production techniques to create the desired effect, which can be particularly dramatic and inventive in contemporary dance. The designer will also be involved in designing the dancer's costumes which may vary from period to fantasy. S/he may use computer-aided design facilities. The designer will probably have related experience e.g. in art, fashion, architecture, film, photography or dance, before going on to do specialist training. You need:

■ Design training
■ Creativity
■ Good visual sense
■ Attention to detail
■ Ability to coordinate visuals with sound/light.

Dance notating

There are two types of notation – Laban and Benesh. Notation is the writing or notating for dance using symbols, much as for music, to convey to the reader the dance movements. This allows the reader to reconstruct the dance by him/herself. The symbols can be very detailed, right down to the use of your toes. Dance notating can be done on computer. It is important to have a genuine interest in dance otherwise you would quickly become uninterested and it would be helpful to have had practical experience. You need:

- Relevant training and qualification
- Dancing experience
- Patience
- Love of dance
- Organisational skills
- To be methodical.

Related occupations

- Stage management and sound
- Dance photography
- Press officer/publicity
- Finance
- Dance support organisations
- Music (dance accompaniment/composition)
- Health and dance (e.g. osteopathy, physiotherapy, psychology)
- Keep fit and exercise
- Enterprise management
- Agent
- Dance company management
- Drama (see above).

The Biz

Josephine Leask, Freelance Writer/Editor

Josephine Leask is a freelance dance critic, but, like many others in her profession has to be flexible within her working environment – she also lectures, choreographs and makes movement-based performance.

Who do you write for?

'I am a freelance writer for various dance magazines. Last summer I covered for the dance critic for *The Independent on Sunday* for a month and may be doing more this year.'

How did you get into dance journalism?

'I did a BA in Dance at Surrey University and our third year was spent doing work experience following our chosen career route, and as I was interested in dance journalism I spent the first four months with the editor of *The Stage* and *Television Today*. When I left university I worked for *Hybrid* magazine doing editorial and subediting, but my main interest was in writing.

'What really launched me was when I did a short course in dance writing at the Dance Umbrella Festival. There are two main dance festivals every year, the Dance Umbrella Festival in the autumn and Spring Loaded. They often run workshops in conjunction with the festivals. In the autumn of '94 I did this short course for dance writers from which I had work published in a newsletter. This was sent to various editors and I then had my first piece of published work in *Ballett International*, which lead to subsequent work.

'I then had other work published in the *Dance Theatre Journal*. I approached different editors and it took off from there. Once you have had work published it becomes easier to get work. I rang up editors, networked and came up with ideas. Once I became familiar they'd commission me. I then went on to edit *Dance UK News*. I had done previous editorial work and worked with editors, so the editing process wasn't completely unfamiliar to me.'

How might someone interested in teaching get into it?

'For higher education you need an MA at least and for universities you normally need a PhD, unless you are going in as a practioner. I got my teaching jobs through networking, word-of-mouth, being seen, talking to other lecturers and heads of departments.'

Any advice for would-be writers?

'There are not many institutes or colleges that do dance journalism. Use all the information that you have gained from your dance courses and then do an MA (not in dance) or journalism course to add to your dance qualifications. It is not enough just to be an experienced dancer and then to start writing on your own. You need help or experience. You need to be broadminded, outward looking and connected to the outside world.'

Chapter 4
SALARIES

Equity negotiates minimum rates for its members and has over 50 industrial agreements across the whole industry which change constantly. Rates for broadcasting are not static, and are dependent on various factors. While there are minimum rates for television work, the actual earnings can vary greatly depending on whether the programme is repeated or sold to overseas broadcasters. As with all acting work, the actual fee for the job depends on how much an actor's agent can negotiate above the minimum. If you need information regarding rates then speak to your agent, call Equity if you are a member or look at their website for the latest minimum rates (see Directory).

Equity recently struck a deal with the Society of West End Theatres that increased actors' and stage managers' pay by six times the rate of inflation. Newcomers to the theatrical profession working on a once-nightly contract who will do eight performances over a six-day week will earn around £320 a week at a West End theatre company, with additional allowance for lodgings if working away from home. Higher rates will be negotiated by agents for more experienced actors, but very few will earn a salary large enough to prevent them seeking alternative forms of employment while 'resting'. The rates for dancers in repertory theatres are the same.

Equity, along with the Theatre Commission, also completed a deal, which began in 1996, for a new pay agreement with subsidised repertory theatre managers. The government has awarded an extra £25 million in public funding for regional theatres, which will become available from 2003.

There are 85 subsidised repertory theatres and companies, all of which will join the Equity pension scheme. This agreement states that the minimum rate for a performer is £300. Stage managers can expect different rates according to the grade of the theatre: grade 1, £370; grade 2, £330; grade 3, £310. Deputy stage managers will receive a minimum of:

grade 1, £330; grade 2, £300; grade 3, £290. The minimum rate for an assistant stage manager will be £275. The minimum rates for allowances include £150 for touring, £105 subsistence for artists living away from home, or £88.58 for artists living more than 25 miles away who choose to commute. Contact Equity for more details.

Musicians' pay, particularly at the start of their careers, may be very low. It is not uncommon for young bands starting out to make a loss after they have paid for a backline tech, driver and travelling costs. Orchestral members may be on standard salary scales or paid per concert. The MU's rate for casual gigs is £45.

Equity/ITC (the Independent Theatre Council) negotiates minimum salaries for dancers which depend on the type, length and location of the work. Contemporary dancers, stage managers and administrators in subsidised productions earn in the region of £200 to £300 a week. Dance teachers in schools and adult education will be paid standard teaching rates. In England and Wales, teachers at state-maintained schools earn in excess of £16,000, while in Scotland the starting salary is about £1000 less. A private teacher will earn about £18 an hour for individual tuition.

Chapter 5
TRAINING

'I did the Saturday School at the Central School of Ballet when I was really young, which was quite a commitment because I lived in Bristol at the time, so it was expensive for my parents and time-consuming too. I did a class with boys taught by men, so I saw the robustness of it. It was taken very seriously.' *Toby Smith, Student on the Professional Course at the Central School of Ballet*

Qualifications in the performing arts can be obtained from the age of five with the graded syllabi for performance training – e.g. Royal Academy of Dancing, Associated Board of the Royal Schools of Music and the Royal Academy of Music and Dramatic Arts – up until postgraduate level (21+).

ACCESS TO HIGHER EDUCATION

In April 2002 national training organisations, such as Metier (arts and entertainment) and Skillset (audio-visual industries) became sector skills councils. Metier and Skillset have set the framework for NVQs in the performing arts. NVQs (National Vocational Qualifications) are now awarded by Edexcel in England and SVQs (Scottish Vocational Qualifications) by SQA in Scotland.

Courses which qualify you up to S/NVQ level are fundamentally a preparation for gaining access to higher education, rather than a direct route into employment in the performing arts. It may also improve your chances of gaining access to competitive professional training courses if you get involved with local performing arts groups such as a local youth theatre group, orchestra or dance production. Access courses are also available for adults, e.g. Access to Theatre, which is good preparation for applying to drama schools.

S/NVQs

There are five different levels of S/NVQ (Scottish/National Vocational Qualifications), from basic (Level 1) to professional (Level 5). S/NVQ assessment is carried out while you are working. Awards are made if you can perform the tasks and meet the standards of competence required. You can train for S/NVQs at your own pace, and any abilities you may already have are recognised without the need for retraining.

There are several S/NVQs pertinent to the performing industry. These are listed below and range from Level 2 to Level 4:

- Teaching
- Visual arts
- Performing arts
- Theatre administration and box office support
- Programming
- Dance
- Technical theatre and arena
- Costume in theatre and arena
- Recording studio sound
- Rigging.

S/NVQs place emphasis on practical skills and a knowledge and understanding of the vocational area of performing arts. Contact Metier (see Directory) for further details.

Foundation Modern Apprenticeship Scheme

Metier has also developed a framework for the Foundation Modern Apprenticeship Scheme in the arts and entertainment sector in England and Wales. This involves the employment of an apprentice by an organisation in the arts and entertainment sector who will receive training and practical experience up to S/NVQ Level 3 and receive a wage. The programme is open to people aged between 16 and 24. This could be someone already working within a relevant organisation, or someone external. If you are interested in the programme, contact your local learning and skills council (LSC) in England and Wales, and local enterprise council (LEC) in Scotland who may be prepared to contribute towards the cost of the training plan over the apprenticeship period. The employer can use this money to finance the training. Contact Metier for more information (details in the Directory).

Professional training

There are four main options for training in the performing arts. These are:

1) Statutory provision, i.e. degrees, postgraduate certificate, diplomas provided by higher and further education colleges and universities.

2) Arts organisations. Some large arts companies will feed some training opportunities to a limited number of individuals. For example, a theatrical company might offer masterclasses to the actors who are working in rep there so they can update their skills. A number of orchestras run their own training for performers to become teachers and animateurs. A dance company might offer injury workshops so their dancers can train to become physiotherapists, for example.

3) Individuals may also provide training in the form of one-to-one private tuition, whether it be in piano, voice or movement.

4) Specialist schools, which provide vocational courses such as dance and drama schools or music conservatoires, e.g. Royal Academy of Dramatic Art (RADA), Laban Centre and the Yehudi Menuhin School offer two- to three-year diploma or degree courses and postgraduate courses for those who have already attended university.

There are also many short courses and summer schools that various organisations can set up including adult education institutes, colleges, universities, arts and independent organisations – though these may not be particularly designed for the professional market – adverts for which you will find in *The Stage* or *Floodlight*. Costs are met by the individual.

The Conservatoire of Dance and Drama

In 2001, a new government initiative dramatically changed the level of funding for talented UK dance and drama students when the Conservatoire of Dance and Drama (CfDD) was established. The CfDD received funding from central government via the Higher Education

Funding Council for England so that all students at the CfDD's affiliate schools will be eligible for funding at a similar level to equivalent UK and EU institutions. Contact the CfDD to find out which institutions are affiliates. Students can be selected on talent alone.

Funding

Sources of funding depend on the type of training you are undertaking.

1) Mandatory grants are available to all music degree and graduate diploma students training in the mandatory sector. You will have to pay tuition fees which are worked out on a sliding scale dependent on your or your parents' income. You also have to pay for your own maintenance costs, for which you may get a student loan. The student loan is paid back after graduation once your annual income reaches a certain level and will probably take several years to pay back. For drama and dance, see above.

2) Discretionary awards: whether you get one of these is completely up to your LEA, as is how much of the tuition fees they choose to pay. They may pay for the full tuition but this is becoming increasingly rare. You will obviously have to make up the shortfall as well as find your maintenance costs.

3) Scholarships and bursaries are distributed from the actual training providers within the independent sector. These are funds to support students of outstanding merit with no alternative sources of financial support. Contact the potential place of study for information and advice.

4) Sponsorships may come from a number of different sources including trusts, foundations, charities, large businesses and famous individuals. The sponsorship tends to be annual so you have to find money for each individual year. You will also need to obtain money for your maintenance costs.

Contact the institution for information on securing funding for your studies, or visit your public library for details of local trusts which may offer awards for educational or cultural development. Alternatively get hold of a copy of Trotman's most recent catalogue for relevant publications on securing funding, applying for a degree and becoming a student. Criteria for eligibility for these awards will vary so it is best to contact the organisations concerned directly.

If you want any information on training in music, drama and dance, contact your Regional Arts Board (RAB) or the National Arts Council and speak to an educational officer (see Directory).

The Metier/Learndirect Helpline is a national learning advice line containing information on careers, course details and learning materials and has a section dedicated to the performing arts. Call the helpline on 0800 093 0444 or visit their website (see Directory).

MUSIC

Places to study include schools of music and music institutions, conservatoires (which offer vocational courses) and universities where you can do combined degrees with music integrated with another subject, e.g. a language or arts management.

Vocational diploma courses for musicians at schools of music and conservatoires generally do not require academic entry qualifications but will require you to have reached grade 8 on your principal instrument and grade 5 on your second, which you will demonstrate at an audition.

Graduate diploma courses are degree equivalents and therefore have academic entry requirements. You will probably be expected to have gained your grade 8 on your principal instrument and grade 6 on your second as well as keyboard skills, which you will be required to demonstrate at an audition. These courses are both practical and theoretical and are run through schools of music and conservatoires. Practically all of these courses have now changed over to actual degree courses.

Degree courses require academic entry qualifications with specialisation in music, unless the course is technology-based, in which case it is useful if you are a musician but not compulsory. You will also have to undergo an audition for performance-based courses, and/or an interview. Degreesare normally taken at colleges and universities, and content may be a lot more academic than vocational. In all cases, it is important to check individual prospectuses before embarking on a course to ensure the training is the kind you are looking for.

Information on music courses

MED – The Music Education Directory, British Phonographic Industry's (BPI) complete guide to contemporary music education, gives detailed information on more than 500 courses run by over 150 colleges and universities that are specifically geared towards providing training in the business, creative and technological sides of the modern music industry throughout the UK. You can browse the website by location, institution or course. Courses range from one-off seminars to postgraduate qualifications. The directory is published annually and is available free from the BPI (or see Directory for website details). *The Degree Course Guide – Music and Drama* (published by Hobson's), which comes out every other year, and the *Complete Guide to Performing Arts Courses*, published annually by UCAS and Trotman will also be worth getting hold of.

CASE STUDY

Rebecca Lacey, Artists' Management Assistant and Classical Musician

Rebecca Lacey is Artists' Management Assistant for Tennant Artists, who manage professional classical musicians, chamber groups and conductors. She is a clarinet player and saxophonist and has played with a saxophone quartet since college – their professional engagements include the Ideal Home Exhibition. Rebecca also works in her spare time for an orchestra, concert-managing several engagements during the course of a year in addition to managing the freelance conductor. This is not all – she also teaches clarinet and saxophone to both children and adults.

What made you go into music?

'My parents were both musical, although they didn't play any instruments we went to a lot of concerts. I always wanted to play and be involved in some capacity. I started playing the recorder when I was eight and then the clarinet and piano and at 16 began to learn the saxophone.'

What's your training background?

'I did all my graded exams. I also did work experience at a local festival. I helped out in the sixth form at school by running music groups and then I went to the London College of Music where I got my GLCM(Hons) [Graduate of the London College of Music (LCM)]. It is now changed to a BMus. The LCM is very performance-based. You have tuition on your main and second instrument and you play in the orchestra and wind band. You are encouraged to go out and set up your own ensembles which is how I became involved in the saxophone quartet. You do other things like music history but a lot of the time is spent playing.

'The LCM really prepares students for going out into the music world too. You learn how to promote yourself and your orchestras. You can also do the Music in Education module where you are given a work placement in a school and you have to prepare lessons. I also did the Psychology of Music module which looked at music therapy.

'I graduated in June 1997 and went straight into my first job. The BBC has a good relationship with LCM and they contacted the college when they were looking for someone to help out at the Proms. The director told me to apply and I got the job.'

How did you get your current job for Tennant Artists?

'It was advertised in the *Guardian* and there were hundreds and hundreds of responses. I think all the other non-paid work experience I had done helped me be selected.'

Any advice?

'However small it seems, get involved, whether it's by going to a local theatre and selling programmes or putting on a concert or helping out at school, this is what your employers will be interested in – the experience – your initiative.'

DRAMA

'The first year was mostly about freeing yourself up, learning to trust people, by playing games, exercises in improvisations, poetry. The second year was about taking risks and pushing yourself. You would be cast against type, playing a character least like you. The final year was purely acting. We put plays on every term and additional agent showings where we performed scenes and songs.'
Gabriella Meara, Student at Central School of Speech and Drama

According to a Manpower Studies report on behalf of the Arts Council of England, 86 per cent of actors working in the industry had professional training. Most of the respondents were happy with the level of careers advice, preparation for work and training they had been given. Recognised drama schools also provide opportunities to be seen by casting directors, agents, theatre and television companies.

The National Council for Drama Training (NCDT) can provide information on accreditation of drama school courses throughout the UK in professional acting, stage management and technical (see Directory). Equity offers full membership to students graduating from courses accredited by the NCDT, without having to first obtain an engagement. The minimum age for two- to three-year courses is 18 and for one-year courses 21. Generally academic entry requirements are not a pre-requisite but an audition and interview are. Degree courses do require the standard academic entry requirements although these may be relaxed for mature students. Degree courses will contain more academic study than the vocational diplomas. If you want to become a fully qualified drama teacher you will need the standard academic entry requirements.

Trainee schemes

Contact local theatres to see if they offer trainee schemes: if they don't yet, maybe you could encourage them to start! Some theatres offer trainee director or trainee adminstrator programmes where you are attached to the theatre for a year, work for free, but get to learn the ropes and work on some productions, e g The Orange Tree Theatre in Richmond. The Graeae Theatre Company also periodically runs admin traineeships for disabled people, in conjunction with the Royal National Theatre, which are coordinated through the Arts Council.

The NCDT provides a database on courses for directors. Aspiring directors, who are over 20, may be offered a placement on the Regional Theatre Young Director Scheme. Details from: RTYDS, PO Box 292, Richmond, Surrey TW9 1FL.

Training schemes for directors are also offered by the Arts Council of England. Contact their drama department for more information.

If teaching drama is what you are interested in, contact the Society of Teachers of Speech and Drama for advice on training (see Directory).

Information on drama courses

The NCDT recommends that all intending actors should complete one of the recognised courses listed in *The Official UK Guide to Drama Training*, available from the Conference of Drama Schools (CDS). See also the *Complete Guide to Performing Arts Courses*, published annually by UCAS and Trotman.

Get online

The website of the Conference of Drama Schools (CDS) also has *The Official UK Guide to Drama Training* online, giving information on the National Council for Drama Training (NCDT) accredited vocational schools.

CASE STUDY

Alison Bullock, Trainee Administration Assistant at the Orange Tree Theatre

At the age of 13, Alison Bullock joined the Epsom Youth Theatre to get more involved with her hobby of acting. She remained with the group until Easter 1997, putting on plays and pantomimes at the Adrian Mann Theatre at Nescott College. After completing her A-levels her head of sixth form advised her to apply for a trainee administration assistant post at the Orange Tree Theatre.

'I had decided to take a year out before going on to university to do a history degree. I didn't really know what I wanted to do in theatre so I wanted to get a job that would give me a wide experience to gain a good background knowledge in order to make a decision. The head of sixth form knew I wanted to work in theatre. Our school had been sent a letter from the Orange Tree Theatre advertising the trainee post. It was a general mail-out letter to most of the schools in Surrey. I think I was selected from about six candidates.'

What does your job entail?

'The job has really grown from when I first started nine months ago. I spend a month in each department; marketing, press, front of house and finance. At the moment I am doing mainly marketing, but I am also working with stage management in The Room. We have two theatres, the pub one and the main house, and I am currently working in the pub theatre and will also be part of the crew for the next production in the main theatre. I will be the assistant stage manager – the one running around in the background dragging props around. This wasn't part of my job description but I was keen to do it. They asked me if I wanted to do it because they knew I wanted to, but I could have said no.'

How long is your contract for?

'My post lasts for a year – from September to September. I was the second trainee administration assistant they had, but they are going to do it every year from now on. They also recruit a couple of trainee directors each year but there are no other trainees here. We get paid our travel expenses. We also have work experience people who come here from time to time. They stay for about two weeks.'

What do you want to go into in the future?

'I'd like to go into stage management ideally, but I might also pursue acting. I shall get involved in acting at university and see how it goes from there. At the moment I don't feel confident enough to do acting.'

What advice would you give to someone who wanted to get into theatre?

'I took this admin job because it's in theatre and I wanted to find out about the theatre and how it worked. If you get offered a job go for it, even if it seems like slightly the wrong area for you, as it will give you a good background so you can find out what you really want to do.'

DANCE

If you want to be a ballet dancer, you will need to audition for a place at one of the big vocational schools to study full-time. Apart from the two famous ballet institutes, the Royal Academy of Dance and the Royal Ballet School, there are a number of dance schools around the UK that offer training from 16 to 18. There are also numerous, smaller dance schools and stage schools which often broaden their curriculums out to include voice, drama, etc.

For dance performance courses you will be expected to undergo an audition which usually involves participating in a class, a health check and possibly a solo performance. For ballet you will probably be required to be no more than 1.65m for a woman and 1.78m for a man. In some cases, for contemporary dance, where performers are less experienced, you may be auditioned so that your suitability and potential for dance can be judged.

In the private sector of dance you are not necessarily required to have specific qualifications for teaching, though this is being positively encouraged, and you will have achieved a high level of dance performance. For those undertaking a degree course to become a qualified teacher you will need the necessary academic entry requirements. In order for a teacher of dance to enter his/her students for the major dance exams (e.g. Royal Academy of Dancing, Cecchetti Society and the Imperial Society of Teachers of Dancing) they must be registered, and in order to register must be qualified, having passed exams in historical, theoretical and of course practical dance.

Degree courses in dance will require the usual academic entry requirements together with some previous dance training. The actual emphasis of practical work involved will vary considerably depending on the institution, so you are advised to always check this with the course director before applying.

You may wish to do a vocationally oriented course in performance or follow a more general programme of study. It is possible to then go on and do a postgraduate course, for example in dance movement therapy or arts administration.

Professional courses for dance commence after leaving school. These independent vocational courses last two to three years and the Council for Dance Education and Training (CDET) can supply you with a list of the accredited schools. They offer degrees, diplomas and certificates. Courses usually include ballet, contemporary and other dance forms as well as choreography, in addition to anatomy, dance notation, history of dance and make-up. Dance courses may offer drama and music to broaden a student's employability.

Information on dance courses

The CDET is the organisation responsible for accrediting dance courses. They will provide you with a list of dance courses in higher education, full-time professional dance training courses and accredited foundation courses. The courses cover the major disciplines of classical ballet, musical theatre and contemporary dance. The actual courses vary in their style, content and aims, so you should always contact the institution directly to ensure you will be getting what you want from the course.

The CDET can also supply you with a list of dance degree courses at universities and colleges around the UK. These courses tend to be less vocational and course content may vary considerably (See also *Performing Arts Courses*, published annually by Trotman.). It is important to check with individual prospectuses and talk to the course director to find out if it is really what you are looking for. Dance UK can also supply you with course information on any other dance-related query.

CASE STUDY

Lucy Butler, Final Year Student, BA in Dance Studies at the University of Surrey, Roehampton

What made you first interested in dance?

'I was a very active child and my mother wanted me to do dance classes, so I started off doing jazz and modern dance combined, once a week when I was four. After the first class the teacher told my mother I was very good and should do ballet, so I started that as well. By the age of seven I knew dancing was what I wanted to do. By the age of eleven I was doing five afternoons a week dancing after school. I was really into it and never missed a class. I got a stress fracture from doing it so much and not eating properly for three years, so my bones had become weak.

'We lived in Trinidad, but every year we came to England in the summer so decided to visit a boarding school that had been recommended to my mother, where you danced and were academically trained too. I really wanted to go, so we looked at different schools and I auditioned for Elmhurst Ballet School and they accepted me.

'I started when I was 11. It was a small school, 350–400 pupils, and we were all very close, with the teachers as well. There was a lot of ballet training and we were streamed in ballet classes. The strong ones had to do more work, pointes, pas de deux, repertoire and so on – which is what I had to do. I was always doing ballet but didn't want to do it professionally. Although ballet has benefited me in the long term because ballet technique is the foundation, I think, of all dance, so you can adapt to any dance. Ballet gives you the strongest training. I left at 16, I needed a fresh start. I was stuck in the ballet category, but wanted to pursue more contemporary dance.

'I went to the London Studio in King's Cross – it was like *Fame* – huge classes, big age ranges. There were ballet classes in the morning and then contemporary or ballet in the afternoon. I was put in top ballet so automatically had to do ballet in the afternoon, but I would say I would rather do jazz. I was there for a year. At Elmhurst, because it was such a family atmosphere, they could see I'd lost my sparkle and ask me what's wrong. At London Studio they would shout at you because that's what it's like in the real world, so I made up my mind at that point that this wasn't for me. I was 17. I started doing my A-levels, and then had my daughter Leah.'

What performances had you taken part in up until this point?

'By the time I left Trinidad I had reached elementary level in the RAD syllabus. At one point five of us were chosen to do the video of the RAD syllabus which was sent around the world. We also had three shows every year – pantomime, musical and dance, which lasted for three weeks and we would perform every night and three matinees.

'Sadler's Wells came to Elmhurst to audition us for their Youth Ballet and I performed around London. We also did *Blue Peter* as part of the promotion for the Sadler's Wells shows. After I had Leah I did some work for a contemporary dance company called Biserk, doing seasonal work, performing in theatres around Oxfordshire, really to help me get on my degree course. I then came to Roehampton to do a BA in Dance Studies combined with Education, because I decided at that point I wanted to be a primary school teacher.

'One of the modules was in performance. We had to do six performances and take the average of our best four marks. We showed them as a performance and the teachers and students voted for the best three from each exam to put in the end-of-year show – and all the pieces I was in were chosen. All the pieces were completely different styles, but I had a lot of positive feedback including a lot of interest from the choreographer from the dance company Retina. I am now thinking about delaying my PGC and following a dance career instead.'

Chapter 6
EQUAL OPPORTUNITIES

Working towards inclusion

Art Skills 2000, a report by Metier – the Sector Skills Council for the arts and entertainment industry – found that 70 per cent of employers believed that, over the next five years, diversity over the arts sector workforce would improve, but were not sure how this would happen. In 2001, Metier received funding of around £5 million to support the removal of barriers to employment for black and minority ethnic people, people with disabilities and to challenge gender stereotyping as part of the Creative Renewal Project. The Department of Culture, Media and Sport will support Metier in these objectives – this is a positive step to eradicating discrimination in the performing arts industry, which unfortunately still exists.

The gender equation

While women occupy a fair proportion of the more secretarial and administrative positions, the music business is still dominated by men, with very few women occupying the more senior roles with power to make decisions.

As for technical grades, you will find some female engineers, lighting technicians etc., but it is unlikely you will spot a woman humping gear on and off stage. Backline technicians tend to be male. On the positive side, orchestras are now made up of a good proportion of women and as they were once mainly male this is a step forward. Female artists, such as Dido and Charlotte Church, have also made a huge impact on record sales.

The theatrical business has, on the whole, good gender representation right up to senior management. The representation of different ethnic groups seems to depend more on locality. While you may not find much representation of different ethnic groups in Richmond, in north London or Kilburn you will.

While dance companies tend to be evenly split between men and women, many more women enter the profession than men, so consequently employment is more competitive. In any audition for a West End show, for every female part there will probably be over 500 women applying, whereas there will be around 50 applicants for every male part.

As far as dance writing is concerned, while there are more women writers now than before, the majority of editors are still male.

Minority ethnic groups

Statistics for 1998–99 showed low representation of black, Asian and Chinese people on the boards and staff of English theatres. As a result the Arts Council of England, the Theatrical Management Association (TMA), East Midlands Arts and Nottingham Playhouse have collaborated to produce the *Eclipse Report* to address institutional racism in theatre. Apart from tackling issues such as employment opportunities and artistic programming, it will also aid the implementation of the arts funding system's National Policy for Theatre which stresses diversity and inclusion (published summer 2000).

While contemporary dance attracts a range of ethnic groups, ballet is predominantly Caucasian, although a fair number of students of Japanese origin do take up ballet. There are also a number of dance companies specialising in different dance cultures such as Adzido (pan-African) and Akademi (South Asian).

Disability

Disabled people are generally under-represented in mainstream music, drama and dance companies, although there are companies with disabled dancers such as CandoCo. CandoCo were based for many years at Laban Centre London and together they developed the first training courses available to disabled dancers.

Laban Centre London recently made a successful application to the National Lottery with a proposal for the creation of a new landmark building, relating to the provision of access for disabled people. Physical access to this building is intended to be exemplary. General opportunities of this new site include MIRC, the Media and Information Resource Centre, which will open up not only the possibility of distance learning, but also the use of technology to allow disabled people to be involved in dance. For example, the development of choreographic software programmes will allow disabled people with limited communication skills to choreograph using computer software, and have dancers perform their work. The Laban Centre has been first in the development of the interface between disabled people and dance, and the development of MIRC will continue this process.

Disability and broadcast

The Broadcasters' Disability Network (BDN) has produced a manifesto to end discrimination against people with disabilities, which includes: to increase the presence of disabled people on the radio and television, increase the number of disabled people working in broadcast and to increase accessibility to services. Equity is talking with BDN on increasing work opportunities for its members. Contact BDN or Equity for further details. One of the BBC's new idents includes a short dance piece by basketball players who are wheelchair users.

Arts access

Lottery money has helped and is helping many theatres, particularly regarding improving access for disabled people. As a result the arts have become far more accessible over the past five years and the National Disability Arts Forum has established Arts Access UK – a free online searchable access guide to arts venues (see Directory).

Greater participation

Greater participation in the arts is encouraged by Vocaleyes. Vocaleyes is a company that can enable blind and visually impaired people to enjoy the performing arts via the use of audio description to enrich the experience. This includes a live verbal commentary, describing the different elements of the show, from the set and characters to facial expression and body language. A pre-production tape is sent in advance of the performance containing information on access, and details of the performance such as characters and costumes, mood and tone. Prior to the actual performance, touch tours are offered which involve access to the stage and feeling the props and costumes. (See Directory, below).

CASE STUDY

Pedro Machado, Dancer with CandoCo

As a dancer with the contemporary dance company CandoCo, Pedro Machado's work stretches far beyond performance. The performers are also involved in coming up with the ideas, designing the piece, rehearsals and giving workshops (with the rest of the group) to disabled and non-disabled people. The seven dancers and the two directors work together to create the dance piece, sometimes using external people.

How did you become a dancer?

'It kind of just happened. I had worked in the theatre in Brazil since I was young and came to London to do mime. Then I found out about the BA in Dance Studies at the Laban Centre and as I had always wanted to do dance decided to apply thinking I would never be accepted. Not only did I get a place but I got a scholarship too. I was 22 which is quite late to start dancing. The course entailed classical and contemporary technique, choreography classes, movement anaylsis, Laban notation, history, etc. It was a very wide course suitable for dancers, teachers and community choreographers.'

How does CandoCo differ from other modern dance companies?

'The fact there are disabled dancers (two of the performers are wheelchair users) makes CandoCo different to begin with, but the company tries to profile CandoCo as a contemporary dance company above everything so as not to label it as a "disabled" or "integrated" company. It is not about disability, although it will be inherent in different degrees within the work but there is no strict reference to it. It is about people and relationships and you cannot distance yourself from the fact they (the wheelchair users) are humans which in one sense might limit the dancers, but also adds a lot of new things that you will never have come across before. Also you get the surprise of detail the wheelchair users can use in their range of work.'

Who are the workshops for?

'Workshops are aimed at anyone. We are open to people with disabilities. What makes us different is that we do not teach the dance technicalities. We are about movement – gaining trust with your partners and finding ways of moving within their capabilities. When we do residencies we choreograph with the people in the group. The workshops are fed by the most recent process. *Out of Here*, the work we are currently on tour with, is directed by the director of theatre de complicite as opposed to a choreographer, and this has influenced the direction taken in our workshops.

'We read poetry (or text, music, imagery, photos, etc.) and visualise what we liked about it and use it in movement. We then divide into three groups and all come up with something completely different. We then make comments on it and rework it. It is very much related to the whole work of the company and the current performance work. The workshops are a great complementary part of the performance work.'

What advice would you offer other people wanting to get into the dance industry?

'With the arts in general there is no job security so you must want it a lot and pursue it a lot. There are dancers who have been very talented who have left because they didn't want it so much and there have been dancers who were not so talented who have wanted to succeed so much they have worked hard and developed their skills, so go for it!'

Chapter 7
GETTING WORK

'Most of the staff here started as interns or work experience people. Get your CV out, visit places and get to know people, because you are more likely to be employed if a lot of people know who you are. Go to gigs, write to record and promotions companies. Offer to do work experience. Be keen, smile, and write everything down. I personally think you've either got it or you haven't – but there's no harm in having a go.' *Eve Delves, Talent and Artist Relations Manager*

You've got the necessary qualifications, you've done some work experience and now all you need is a job, but how do you go about securing work?

Where are jobs advertised?

Music jobs are advertised in the music and trade press, including *Classical Music*, *Music Journal*, and *NME*, and music teaching jobs in *Music Teacher* and the *Times Educational Supplement*.

You will also find performing arts jobs in the recruitment section of *The Stage*. This is a weekly trade paper for every sector of the entertainment industry and has a website which details a weekly roundup of the 'jobs of the week'. This includes the major auditions going on in the UK, but you will need to get hold of a copy of the paper for all the details.

Actors should consider putting their details and photographs in *The Spotlight*, a casting database of professional actors for the theatre, television and film industries. It is available as a book, on CD-ROM and online. *Production and Casting Report* and *Repertory Report* are other ways of finding out who is casting for new productions.

The Place Dance Services publishes a newsletter for its members entitled *Juice*, which amongst other things gives information on auditions and jobs. They can also help you if you want to set up your own dance company, etc.

Look at the trade press (see Directory) or look in the current *Writers' and Artists' Yearbook*, published by A&C Black (see p111 for details) for a list of newspapers and magazines published nationally and internationally which might be of use.

Get online and check out websites which have jobs noticeboards (see Directory).

Metier, the membership organisation established by and for the arts and entertainment sector, can provide careers information at both entry level and for graduates, using the Internet to gain the most up-to-date information. Metier's remit includes: arts administration and management, arts development and teaching, performing arts, technical stagecrafts and support areas, visual art and crafts and writing.

Metier works closely with freelance practitioners and larger organisations and employers. It also runs the Modern Apprenticeship Scheme and is introducing the National Traineeships. (See Training chapter).

Get in direct contact and ask to audition with orchestras, theatre companies or dance companies. They sometimes offer freelance work. Enterprising young people may set up their own ensemble, theatre or dance company and get paid for performances and gain valuable experience. You obviously need to have reached a high standard of craftsmanship and know how to market your talent. Young dancers and actors and crew can also set up their own company. Dancers get in contact with the Place Dance Services for useful information and advice. The Arts Council and regional arts boards provide some funds to commission new works. Development funds are also available to support the production, distribution and development of specific projects and research. Contact the Library and Enquiry Service at the Arts Council of England for a leaflet about these support funds.

You might also like to contact broadcasting organisations to find out what the opportunities are for getting your music used in soundtracks. Essentially you need to study and target your work, researching the current requirements. You need to be aware that little unpublished music is used, so approaching a reputable music publisher should probably be your first line of enquiry.

Agencies

Another way to get a foot in the door of the music industry is through agency recruitment. Handle (www.handle.co.uk) is the most well-known agency, specialising in placing temporary and permanent workers in music companies. The agency is primarily for secretaries but also offers more senior posts too such as production managers, promotions, etc. As you might well guess they have hundreds of names on their books, but if you want to give them a try you will need secretarial/keyboard and IT skills and probably a degree if you want to break into the classical side of music. Agents also exist for musicians, actors, dancers and technicians. Find yourself a reputable one and let them find you work. Look in the *British Theatre Directory* for a list of agents.

For those of you more interested in getting into the business side of music you need to get in whatever way you can, whether it be as a receptionist, assistant engineer or a general dogsbody. Don't worry if the record company that offers you your first job or work experience doesn't put out the kind of music you're into. Take whatever you can because wedging your foot firmly in that door is what counts at this stage and it's all good experience to add to your CV.

Alternatively offer to scout bands for a record company as work experience, they may take you up and offer you your expenses too. Or hang around venues and bands that look like they might get signed and offer to help out in whatever way you can. Getting known and making contacts is the best way to get on in the music industry.

Writers

Would-be music, drama or dance journalists or publicists should be writing as much as they can. Putting out a fanzine or writing for your school or college magazine is all good experience and evidence of your commitment. Then think about a suitable journalism course which will both benefit your writing and give you industry recognition. Write reviews of the gigs/concerts you go to and send them to the reviews editor of a suitable publication making sure you write in a similar style and about the kind of music that would be published in their magazine.

The Biz

Ian Harvey, Agent, Focus Management

Focus Management has been established since 1982 and is an agency for actors in theatre, television, film, radio, commercials, corporate videos and personal appearances as well as for some technicians (camera operators, make-up artists etc.) in film and television. Names on their books include Arthur Bostram from *'Allo 'Allo* and Mina Anwar from the *Thin Blue Line*. They also started off Tim Roth on his career path.

How do you recruit people on to your books?

'We visit drama schools, get recommendations, sometimes, funnily enough, from other agencies. People write in telling us of productions they are in and if we are interested we go and see them. This is dependent on our current client list, i.e. if there is a gap – if we need someone on our books who can play cello for example – or the actor has outstanding qualities or is multi-talented – a singer, actor and a musician.'

What do you look for when recruiting?

'Not one thing in particular. Excellent musical skills are always useful – not just the piano but string or brass – pop musicians too as there are a lot of rock and roll musicals.'

Do they have to be Equity members?

'No one has to be an Equity member any more since 1991 when it was illegal to say you had to be a union member. Closed shops became illegal. Although this is the theory it still exists in practice to an extent. There are still some companies that are unlikely to take on non-Equity members. If someone is particularly good and is not an Equity member it is unlikely to be a problem, but for someone who is run-of-the-mill it may be more of a problem. You do need Equity for certain circumstances such as negotiating contracts. Equity are currently having a dispute concerning the commercial production companies who are saying they don't need Equity members and are using anyone off the streets and it shows.'

What advice would you give to someone wanting to get on your books?

'Be brilliant. Be different. Have a unique selling point. Also there is a fine line between hassling someone and alerting someone to your presence. Unfortunately this varies from day to day. If an agent is very busy with lots of telephone calls trying to get work, and after all this is the job of an agent, it is not a good day. The best way is to write in with a CV and photo and an SAE (stamped addressed envelope) because if you don't enclose a SAE you won't get a reply. If people do phone up I try and be polite but get them off the phone as quickly as possible telling them to write in and that we'll get back to them if we are interested. We also never take on anyone without seeing their work first.'

What advice would you give to someone who wanted to be an agent?

'It is a horrible job. You are the bumwiper, the shoulder to cry on, the moral support. I used to be an actor and when I gave that up to become an agent I though great, no more auditions, but now I have to do it 45 times as much – as that's the number of clients we have on our books – and get all the heartache.'

What percentages do agents take?

'We have a split scale – ten per cent for theatre and radio and 15 per cent for everything else, which is fairly near the norm although it varies between two and a half per cent to some personal managers who take 25 per cent.'

Chapter 8
CVs, INTERVIEWS AND
AUDITIONS

'We have about 500 CVs on file which we've kept because they've stood out. They have demonstrated they're into music, possibly a little bit quirky too. I picked our current intern because he said he liked *Star Trek*, there was a spark and he was a total music anorak Some people apply for jobs – they don't know what they want to do, but they want a job. They don't have any particular music interest, they don't know what a record company does and they don't have any nous. They haven't bothered to research MTV at all. I don't want to know – I just don't have the time. From the 500 CVs I've gone through I've picked six for interview.' *Eve Delves, Talent and Artist Relations Manager, MTV UK*

Your curriculum vitae

The content and presentation of your CV is vitally important in getting you work or work experience. All jobs in the performing arts are highly competitive, so the people responsible for reading your CV will be reading hundreds of others. Therefore keep it brief and concise – it is best to keep your CV to one side of A4 only. Although this may seem impossible, the person reading your CV does not want to know the intimate details of every Saturday job you've ever done, or all the hobbies you are interested in – unless of course these are directly relevant. Also if you avoid narrative in writing your CV and use key words instead it will sound more professional too. Remember it must be short and have impact.

Employment history and work experience and training

After your personal details – name, address, telephone number and date of birth – you can put your qualifications and employment history.

Include any work experience under this section. Any evidence you can provide of your commitment to the industry is vital. Also include competition prizes and awards, who you trained with, etc.

Skills and attributes

If you do not have work experience – you may even be applying to get work experience – sell yourself by writing down the transferable and specialised skills you've acquired, such as typing, horse-riding or grade 7 piano, and the personal qualities you can offer such as efficiency and a vital sense of humour! Include what instruments you can play or any other relevant skills.

Tailoring your CV

Don't write a standard CV and think that's it. You must always write your CV according to the job for which you are applying. A theatre company recruiting a publicist will be looking for different attributes from a record company recruiting a receptionist.

The most fundamental thing your CV should achieve is to make the interviewer want to meet you. Well-written CVs are essential in this competitive industry, not only for writing to prospective employers, but also if you are applying for a trainee scheme or work experience. You must present and market yourself professionally, so being able to put yourself across well on paper is vital. Performers should also include a decent photograph of themselves.

The criteria

Of course the majority of jobs in performing arts are not advertised. Many are filled through networking or internal shifting, so it is always good to keep in touch with what is going on in the industry if you can. When you do see a job vacancy or training scheme listed in the paper, check the criteria the successful applicant must match, e.g. previous box office experience. Only apply if you fulfil the criteria because you will be wasting your time if you don't, as there will be plenty who do. If you do match the criteria make sure you highlight these things about yourself in your covering letter.

Do your research

Always do your research on the company you are applying to. It is essential you know as much about the company as possible so you can discuss knowledgeably with your interviewer such things as their mission statement, productions they have put on in the past or artists they have on their label. Likewise, musicians approaching record companies should know what kind of music is on their label and who they most recently signed. It is only worth approaching those companies that put out similar music to yours.

Auditions

> 'The audition I had to do was horrible. It was from *Dangerous Liaisons* and I had to straddle a chair and speak the lines of a French prostitute and blow smoke in the face of the course director in front of a room full of people. It was very intimidating.' *Alice Brickwood, Actor*

If it is an audition you are going for find out exactly what the casting director is looking for and make sure you fit that part down to the minutest detail – clothes, hair, make-up, accent and attitude. Go to the library and read the play (if it has already been published). It is important you know the part you are going for and in what period/style the director is putting it on, so you will fulfil his/her criteria as closely as possible. Dancers should find out a bit about the background of the company and the style the choreographer works in. You need to be prepared and professional. Is the audition open, invitation only or do you need to register?

Why do you think you should get the job?

Be prepared to discuss your CV (you might well be asked to explain what you mean when you say you are 'well organised') and don't forget to be prepared for the most important question of all, 'Why do you think you should get the job?'

CASE STUDY

Annie Carpenter, Actor

What first made you interested in acting?

'I chose GCSE Drama at school and loved it. I soon had to make a decision between studying performing arts at college or pursuing the safer option of something like Business Studies. Studying drama gave me a sudden and unexpected chance to break away from all previously held expectations and find my individuality.'

What qualifications did you get after your GCSE in drama?

'I did BTEC Performing Arts, Theatre Studies A level and BA (Hons) in Dramatic Arts.'

What work have you done, paid or unpaid?

'I have been involved in all sorts of work since finishing at school. Everything from plays at local and fringe theatres, parts in travelling shows, appearances in shows at festivals, and presenting work both on TV and video.'

What are auditions like?

'Auditions are like a mixture of excitement and nerves. I find that the more professional the jobs the less they ask you to do and vice versa. Make sure you have two or three speeches that you enjoy and get extra singing lessons as early as possible. The more skills that you have to offer the better.'

What are the pros and cons of acting?

'The pros are that when you work it is always fun and challenging. You can follow your dream and keep learning, and you are never in the same place – you are constantly working with different people. The cons are that there are too many actors and not enough jobs. You need to be constantly striving and active in all respects because if you stop you can grind to a halt. It is a cliché, but the rejection is very difficult to deal with. You have to make a real effort not to take rejection personally. It is also important to realise at an early stage that acting is like being a sportsman. It is just as competitive and if you are not a naturally competitive person then it can grind you down.'

How do you support yourself financially when not working as an actor?

'I have done many jobs from waitressing, bar work, managing a shop and temping work. You will have to do things to supplement your income. I now work at a recording studio and a yoga centre, both part-time. I have to live within my means at present and cannot afford the level of material wealth of many of my full-time job peers.'

Any advice?

'Be 100 per cent sure that is what you want to do. You have to be constantly motivated. Try to decide which specific area you wish to pursue. If it is purely acting then try for a drama school if possible. If it is performing, teaching and acting, drama-related professions, then there are some fantastic university degree courses. Be prepared for rejection and disappointment. It happens to the best of actors, and you will experience constant rejection and criticism. Don't take it personally, don't give up, believe in yourself and don't take no for an answer! Good luck.'

The Biz

Adrian McKinney, Catalogue Development Manager at Universal

Adrian McKinney's work involves making creative use of the Universal Music Catalogue – placing songs in film, advertisements and TV shows etc. He originally started out working for EMI's tape library at Abbey Road Studios. After several years working as a tape librarian, Adrian left to work for EMI Premier, where he supervised the soundtrack for the film *Mojo*, which was produced by Portobello Pictures. He was then headhunted by Eric Abraham, Director of Portobello Pictures, to set up and run the Itchy Teeth label, trading through Portobello Pictures, as A&R Manager. As A&R Manager, it was Adrian's job to discover new talent to produce music to sell to the public.

What did your job as A&R Manager entail?

'It involves finding acts, organising the recording of a demo then a first single. The DAT (digital audio tape) master copy of the single is then taken to the distributor who will give it to the manufacturer to produce a run of around 5000 CDs. The distributor's in-house designer will design the CD sleeve. The CD will be marketed either by the distributors in-house team or by another independent source. A plugger will sell the music to the different media (press, radio, tv, etc.) and telesales staff will sell to the shops. Once the CD is sold, the profits will be divided so that the distributor takes a percentage and the act receives a royalty. This is how the money is made, although initially it is likely that independent record companies will make a loss or break even if they sell out of their first run.'

How did you find new talent?

'By trawling around a lot of pretty awful gigs. We also had a permanent advert in the *NME* asking for demos. We got about two a day, but most of these demos come from word-of-mouth and personal contacts. We also got demos from publishers and lawyers.'

So bands actually get lawyers before they get a deal?

'Yes, these days a music/media lawyer almost acts like an A&R person and sometimes as a manager too. A band will get a lawyer and the lawyer will get them the deal. It is more usual for a band to have a manager before a lawyer, but it is not unheard of for the lawyer to be involved first. It's also in the lawyer's financial interest to get the act a deal.'

What did you look for in an act?

'I looked for original, innovative music – at least two strong songs – a good look or image. The band must look young too unfortunately, although you can be older for dance music because it's faceless.'

What advice would you give to people wanting to break into the industry?

'Be prepared to work for nothing or low pay initially for long hours. Be totally aware of what's going on. Listen to the radio, read the music papers, go to gigs, talk to people, go to the smaller gigs and get involved with emerging bands from an early stage. It's good to get work experience, but don't expect to be employed. Someone wanting to become a studio engineer should definitely get work experience making tea and helping out the engineer or you can act as a scout looking for bands and get just your expenses paid.'

Chapter 9
SUMMARY

If, having read this far, you are still determined to achieve a career in the performing arts consider these final points:

- Check the attributes listed under the relevant section. Consider your own skills and personality and assess whether you really are suited to a job in music, drama or dance.
- Make yourself as knowledgeable as possible about the performing arts area you want to go into. Read as much as you can, contact useful organisations, try and speak to someone already doing what you would like to do.
- Focus yourself on achieving your career goal.
- Do as much as you can to enhance your employability by gaining relevant skills through professional training, NVQs, degrees and postgraduate courses.
- Get as much work experience wherever and whenever you can. Organise your own concerts or productions as evidence of your self-motivation and commitment.
- Write a concise CV that markets you effectively. Include a decent photo, newspaper reviews, demo tape, etc. where applicable.
- Make and maintain contacts in the industry, write in to and call up companies and follow up any response you receive.
- Keep an eye on the relevant publications and get online to keep yourself up-to-date and knowledgeable about the performing arts industry so you don't miss out on any advertised job, audition, trainee opportunities.
- Maintain your enthusiasm and don't let rejections put you off. Keep a flexible approach.

Do all of the above, be persistent, and you stand a better chance of getting in and getting on. Good luck!

The Biz

Matthew Napier, Production Manager, BBC Children's Drama

Matthew Napier works as a Production Manager at the BBC and as a First Assistant Director at ITV and in films, 'which is more or less the same job'.

How do you get people for castings?

'Initially we send out a cast breakdown – a list of the principal parts of the production – to about ten agents. The cast breakdown will say for example, Micky, father of the hero, 40 years old, a lorry driver with aspirations to do better things. They then send you ideas of who they've thought will be good for the part and you, the producer and the director select the ones you think will be suitable for the casting. You meet with them, they talk a bit about themselves and what they have been doing and then they read a bit of the script and depending on their suitability, ability and availability you take them.

'In films they have a casting director who is responsible for doing the initial suggestions for casting. They go out and see lots of plays and go to as many drama schools to see productions as they can, so they can invest their experience into your project. Casting is such a key element to a production. It is vital that you get it right.'

What criteria do you use in casting?

'Until that person walks in and is right for the part it is hard to lay down the exact criteria. For example, you might want someone in their early 40s who's tall, dark and handsome, and see 50 actors matching that description, but apart from the basic description there's that extra something which is difficult to define, and sometimes only one person would have. Occasionally you know instantly someone is right for the part and once you've ensured they sound right and can act you think, "Bingo!". But if they can't act they won't get the part. You rarely find anyone that matches your ideal 100 per cent, but you will find someone very near to it, about 70–80 per cent, but they may give you 20–30 per cent of something different which allows you to mould the part to fit the actor to ensure a totally convincing character or trait.'

What particular qualities, skills or training do you look for?

'When we are doing castings we always check CVs. This contains information such as eye colour, height, a photo and useful other attributes such as whether they can ride a horse or not, but we do also take relevant qualifications into consideration, like whether someone has been to drama school or not. It almost acts as a back-up to the reason we might have chosen them. For example we might look at their experience of television work and theatre. They may have done theatre work but not done any TV. If you're casting for TV you'd rather look for someone with TV drama experience – such as a few episodes of *Ballykissangel* or *Peak Practice* and also if they have spent a period at the Royal Shakespeare Company they must be able to act! You are more likely to bring them in for a casting because you know they have worked on some good drama and can "do" television.'

What advice would you give to young people trying to break into television drama?

'It's a long road from the desire to the fulfilment of that desire, but if you are committed and talented enough you will get there in the end. Anyone in two minds, I suspect, will not, because you have to face a lot of rejection.'

The Biz

Peter Lawrence, Director of The Big Chill

How did you begin your music career?

'Music was in my family. My dad was a jazz drummer. I sort of fell into the business almost by default. My training involved three years working in a record shop (Our Price Records) which gave me an incredible musical training, a good understanding of distribution and marketing techniques of major labels, hyping, etc, and also of retail and people management. Through this job I got to know a specialist music distributor and so I became a Sales Manager for Making Waves Distribution. In 1986 I set up the label Cooking Vinyl Records, which was my first self-employed job, and four years later I started up another business, *On Magazine* with independent publishers. Then in 1994, I became director of The Big Chill, which is a festival, club events label.'

What sort of criteria do you look for when taking someone on to work for you?

'A whole variety. Enthusiasm and understanding of the job, attractive personality, initiative and intelligence.'

What are the pros and cons of working in this business?

'The pros are that it is a dynamic industry, with plenty of room for maverick characters. It is exciting, global and forever following new directions. The cons are that it is full of sharks, still largely an old boy network and run by faceless majors that are stifling its creativity, and unimaginative retail outlets that are not fulfilling their sales potential.'

How has the music industry changed since you began working in it?

'It has changed in many ways, not least that there is less room for creative enthusiasts and it is more run by accountants wanting successful results. It is much harder for independents to survive and harder to remain outside formatting.'

Any advice?

'Be alert. Read and listen. Be humble. Connect but don't be pushy. This business is so much about inter-personal relations and PR. Keep your eyes and ears open. Follow your heart.'

The Biz

Marguerite Porter, Senior Principal Ballerina for the Royal Ballet in 1978

Marguerite Porter joined the Royal Ballet in 1966. She toured for a year with the Royal Ballet in 1971 to develop her strength by doing a lot of performances and returned to do many solo performances. In 1976 she became the principal dancer and two years later the senior principal dancer. She left the Royal Ballet in 1985, but returned as a guest artist for the following two years. Marguerite is still dancing today, her most recent performance being as the principal dancer in *On Your Toes* at the Haymarket Theatre in Leicester.

'It's a very, very difficult life, and that is an understatement. You can choose the option that you just love to dance, that you love to do ballet and you don't care if you just stay in the corps de ballet because as long as you dance you are happy. Lots of dancers have this attitude and don't mind if they stay in the corps de ballet. But to become a senior ballerina is very, very, very difficult. You need to have so many attributes: you must have the physical shape, you need the strength and stamina and the tenacity to hang in there. And there is the physical pain – it hurts! It is a very difficult life. If you have to do it, do it, but if you don't, do something else.'

DIRECTORY

FURTHER READING

A Dancer's Survival Guide, Dance UK (see Organisations, below)

ABTT Careers in Technical Theatre: So you want to work backstage? available (online only) from the Association of British Theatre Technicians website: www.abtt.org.uk/train/workin.html

An Introduction to Music Therapy/A Career in Music Therapy/ Employment published by the Association of Music Therapists (see Organisations, below)

Fit to Dance? Report of the national enquiry into dancers health and injuries. Dr Peter Brinson and Fiona Dick, Calouste Gulbenkin Foundation, London

How to be a Working Actor, James Duke, Virgin Publishing Ltd

How to Make it in the Music Business, Sian Pattenden, Virgin Publishing Ltd

Questions and Answers: Theatre and Drama and *Music*, Trotman

Stage Management and Theatre Administration, Pauline Mcnear and Terry Hawkins, Phaidon

Stage Management and Theatrecraft, Routledge

Music Making and Disabled People, Sound Sense (see Organisations, below)

The Rock File – Making It In The Music Business, Oxford University Press

Association of Graduate Careers Advisory Services (AGCAS) publishes a list of Careers Information booklets, including:

Broadcasting Film, Video and Theatre

Job Seeking After Graduation (helpful advice on constructing your CV and how to prepare for interviews).

Performing Arts and Arts Administration

Teaching in Schools and Colleges in the UK

For other books on education, careers and the performing arts, go to the Trotman website: www.careers-portal.co.uk

DIRECTORIES/GUIDES

British and International Music Yearbook Directory of British Classical Music, features artists and agents, venues, promoters, organisations, education, suppliers etc., Rhinegold Publishing

The British Performing Arts Yearbook, Rhinegold Publishing

Contacts, directory of all the people or companies you might need to know in stage, television, film and radio. Available from *Spotlight* (see below)

Music Education Directory, information on music courses throughout the UK, also at www.bpi-med.co.uk (BPI) (see Organisations, below)

Musicians' Handbook, Rhinegold Publishing

Performing Arts Courses, annual guide to courses in dance, drama, music, performing arts and other related subjects, UCAS & Trotman

Performing Arts Yearbook for Europe, Arts Publishing International Ltd

Showcase International Music Business Book, Showcase Publications

Spotlight, profiles and photographs of professional actors also available as quarterly CDs and as Spotlight interactive. Casting directory for the theatre, television and film industries. 7 Leicester Place, London WC2H 7BP. Tel: 020 7437 7631, website: www.spotlightcd.com

The UK Guide to Drama Training, describes the courses offered by the 21 Conference of Drama schools.

The White Book, information on record, concert, entertainment and media industries. Studio 27, Shepperton Studios, Studios Road, Shepperton, Middlesex TW17 0DQ. Tel: 01932 572 622, website: www.whitebook.co.uk

Writers' and Artists' Yearbook, A&C Black

www.stageregister.com, the register of independent full-time and part-time stage and drama schools in the UK.

MAGAZINES AND EZINES

Animated, quarterly magazine of the Foundation of Community Dance, 13–15 Belvoir Street, Leicester LE1 6SL. Tel: 0116 275 5057

Classical Music, industry news and classical music – jobs, notice-board every fortnight. Rhinegold Publishing

DAIL: Disability Arts in London, monthly magazine with latest news and views, comprehensive listing of events and opportunities. 34 Osnaburgh Street, London NW1 3ND. Tel: 020 7916 6351

Dance Europe, auditions, jobs, where to study in Europe, reviews and courses. PO Box 12661, London E5 9TZ. Tel: 020 8985 7767

Dance Gazette, published by the Royal Academy of Dancing – a membership magazine about the work of the Academy. It is available to buy if you visit the Academy, and would make a useful read for those interested in going into dance teaching as the RAD claims to be the main dance teacher training organisation in the world. Tel: 020 7326 8000, fax: 020 7924 3129

Dance Now, covers all areas of dance, 'stimulating, controversial, incisive and witty'. Produced quarterly, annual subscription is £10. Dance Books

Dance Theatre Journal, contemporary dance magazine, recommended for dance artists, students, teachers or dedicated members of the audience. Laban Centre (see Useful Addresses, below)

Dancing Times, the Dancing Times Ltd Monthly magazine, international and UK listings, reviews, technical features, reviews. Email: dt@dancing-times.co.uk

Dance UK News, national and international listings information on conferences, courses and publications. The Healthier Dancer Supplement publishes latest news and research which underpins the work of the Healthier Dance Programme. Dance UK (see Organisations, below)

Dotmusic.com, Internet site covering all genres of music from pop and hip hop to classical. Website: www.dotmusic.com

Intermusic.com, Ezine for people who make music. Website: www.intermusic.com

International Arts Manager, Arts Publishing International Limited

Making Music Demonology, Making Music, WViP, Hightgate Studios, 53-79 Highgate Road, London NW5 1TW. Email: editor.music@nexusmedia.com

Mi2n Music Industry News Network, news and information. Website: www.mi2n.com

Music Magazine Monthly, classical magazine in Braille and on disk – reviews, teaching technique, articles. RNIB (see Organisations, below)

Music Monthly, classical music magazine with reviews and listings. BBC, tel: 020 8433 3283, email: music.magazine@bbc.co.uk

Music Teacher, News of courses, seminars, music technology, tips on instrumental teaching. Rhinegold Publishing

Muzik, dance music monthly magazine published by IPC. It is subheaded 'the new testament to club culture' and contains features on individuals in the industry with a news, chart and classified section. IPC Media

NME, weekly music paper, reviews, listings, interviews and classifieds. Website: www.nme.com. IPC Media

Opera Now is a professional magazine with features on opera companies and singers, reviews of world wide operas, profiles of people in the business and a recruitment section. Tel: 020 7333 1740

PCR: Production and Casting Report, weekly film, TV and theatre publication – what's in preproduction, development and casting. PO Box 100, Broadstairs, Kent T10 1UJ. Tel: 01843 860885

Scene4, international magazine of theatre, film and media. Production notebooks, plays, scripts, interviews etc. Email: editor@scene4.com

The Stage, entertainment trade weekly covering every sector of the entertainment industry – news, reviews, features and advertising. Also *The Stage* website featuring 'jobs of the week' including major UK auditions. 47 Bermondsey Street, London SE1 3XT. Tel: 020 7357 9287. Website: www.thestage.co.uk, email: editor@thestage.co.uk

Ssinfo, monthly community music electronic bulletin of news and diary dates. Sound Sense (see Organisations, below)

Studio Sound Professional, technical, pro audio business magazine, featuring articles on recording, post production and broadcast sound. Studio Sound is a must-read for anyone interested in the engineering process, as it not only contains information concerning the most up-to-date technological advances in studio development but also advertises job vacancies. CMP Information, 7th floor, Ludgate House, 245 Blackfriars Road, London SE1 9UR. Tel: 020 7940 8500, fax: 020 7407 7102, email: tgoodyer@cmpinformation.com

Upbeat, available in Braille and on disk – rock, pop, jazz, folk and more – listings, reviews and interviews. RNIB (see Organisations, below)

ORGANISATIONS

Akademi, South Asian Dance in the UK Training, education, community, resources and information. Hampstead Town Hall, 213 Haverstock Hill, London NW3 4QP. Tel: 020 7691 3210, fax: 020 7691 3211, website: www.akademi.co.uk, email: admin@akademi.co.uk

aetti: Arts and Entertainment Technical Training Initiative Lower Ground, 14 Blenheim Terrace, London NW8 0EB, email: aetti@sumack.freeserve.co.uk

Arts Council of England 14 Great Peter Street, London SW1P 3NQ. Tel: 020 7333 0100, website: www.artscouncil.org.uk

Arts Council of Wales Holst House, 9 Museum Place, Cardiff CF10 3NX. Tel: 029 2037 6500, website: www.ccc-acw.org.uk, email: information@ccc-acw.org.uk

Arts Council of Wales South East Wales Office, Victoria Street, Cwmbran. Tel: 01633 875075

Arts Line Information service on access to the arts. 54 Chalton Street, Camden, London NW1 1HS. Tel: 020 7388 2227 fax: 020 7383 2653, text: 020 7383 2653, website: www.artsline@org.uk, email: access@artsline.org.uk

ABTT: Association of British Theatre Technicians Publications, information, training etc. Student membership £10. 47 Bermondsey Street, London SE1 3XT. Tel: 020 7403 3778, website: www.abtt.org.uk/intro.htm, email: office@abtt.org.uk

APMT: Association of Professional Music Therapists 26 Hamlyn Road, Glastonbury, Somerset BA6 8HT. Tel: 01458 834919, website: www.apmt.org.uk, email: apmtoffice@aol.com

APRS: Association of Professional Recording Services Encompasses professional audio from traditional music studios to new generation of project studios, to post-production and broadcast, live sound, film soundtracks and duplication to training and education. (Some centres of learning are educational members of APRS.) 2 Windsor Square, Silver Street, Reading, Berks RG1 2TH. Website: www.aprs.co.uk, email: info@aprs.co.uk

BBC Information PO Box 1922, Glasgow G2 3WT. Tel: 08700 100222, email: info@bbc.co.uk

British Academy of Composers and Songwriters Music writers of all genres – information, advice, support and awards. British Music House, 26 Bermers Street, London W1T 3LR. Tel: 020 7636 2929, fax: 020 7636 2212, email: info@britishacademy.com, website: www.britishacademy.com

British Music Information Centre Promotion and documentation resource for contemporary British music, open to public 12-5pm,

Monday to Friday and is free. Sample scores and recordings freely available to browse through their website. 10 Stratford Place, London W1C 1BA. Tel: 020 7499 8567, fax: 020 7499 4795, email: info@bmic.co.uk, website: www.bmic.co.uk

British Performing Arts Medicine Trust Provides appropriate practitioners for performers. 196 Shaftesbury Avenue, London WC2H 8JF. Tel: 020 7240 3331, website: www.bpamt.co.dial.pipex.com, email: bpamt@dial.pipex.com

BPI: British Phonographic Industry 25 Savile Row, London W15 2ES. Tel: 020 7851 4000, fax: 020 7851 4010, website: www.bpi.co.uk, email: general@bpi.co.uk

BSMT: British Society for Music Therapy Membership to anyone interested in music therapy and reduced rate £23 per annum for full-time students. Publishes the *British Journal of Music Therapy* and *BSMT Bulletin*. 25 Rosslyn Avenue, E Barnet, Herts, EN4 8DH. Tel/fax: 020 8368 8879, website: www.bsmt.org, email: info@bsmt.org

CDS: Conference of Drama Schools Encourages the highest standards in training for both actors and stage managers as well as hosting a variety of associated training in related technical and media studies in the UK. Check their website for information on drama schools and their *UK Guide to Drama Training*. 1 Stanley Avenue, Thorpe, Norwich NR7 0BE. Website: www.drama.ac.uk, email: enquiries@cds.drama.ac.uk

CDET: Council for Dance Education and Training For information on dance training and a list of accredited courses (including those for children) contact Studio 8, The Glasshouse, 49A Goldhawk Road, London W12. Tel: 020 7247 4030, fax: 020 7247 3404, website: www.cdet.org.uk, email: info:cdet.org.uk

COMA: Contemporary Music-Making for Amateurs Promotes participation for musicians of all abilities, in contemporary music. COMA commissions challenging works from leading UK and international composers, suited to the technical abilities of amateur ensembles, and provides opportunities to participate in all aspects of music making. Toynbee Studios, 28 Commercial Street, London E1

6LS. Tel: 020 7247 7736, fax: 020 7247 7732, website: www.coma.org, email: coma@coma.org

Dance UK is a nationally recognised support and development agency for dance, set up for and by the profession to listen to its concerns and take action on its behalf. Dance UK encompasses all of the different dance forms including ballet, contemporary and non-western dance. Register of medical and complementary practitioners to treat dancers. Battersea Arts Centre, Lavender Hill, London SW11 5TN. Tel: 020 7228 4990, fax: 020 7223 0074. Website: www.danceuk.org, email: info@danceuk.org

Equity: British Actors' Equity Association Trade union representing performers in arts and entertainment including actors, singers, dancers, choreographers, stage managers, theatre designers and directors, TV and radio presenters. List of jobs can be accessed on Equity website by members only. Information leaflet *How to Join Equity* Guild House, Upper St Martins Lane, London WC2H 9EG. Tel: 020 7379 6000, website: www.equity.org.uk, email: info@equity.co.org.uk

European Network of Information Centres for the Performing Arts There are 23 member information centres around Europe. ENCIPA's goal is to make avialable all information on performing arts (excluding music) to professionals. Leroy House, 436 Essex Road, London N1 3QP. Tel: 020 7226 8181, website: www.encipa.org

Foundation of Community Dance National development agency and lead-body providing information and support, professional development, advocacy and representation. They publish *Network News* every fortnight. Cathedral Chambers, 2 Peacock Lane, Leicester LE1 5PX, Tel: 0116 251 0516, fax: 0116 251 0517, website: www.communitydance.org.uk, email: info@communitydance.org.uk

Guild of Songwriters and Composers International organisation. Members are songwriters, composers, musicians, publishers, studio owners etc. Offers advice and assistance on how to promote songs to music publishers, legal advice and who requires songs for publishing and recording. Sovereign House, 12 Trewartha Road, Praa Sands, Penzance, Cornwall TR20 9ST. Tel: 01736 762826, fax: 01736 763328, website: www.songwriters-guild.co.uk, email: songmag@aol.com

Incorporated Society of Musicians 10 Stratford Place, London W1C 1AA. Tel: 020 7629 4413, fax: 020 7408 1538, website: www.ism.org, email: membership@ism.org

Independent Theatre Council 12 Leathermarket, Weston Street, SE1 3ER. Tel: 020 7403 1727

International Dance Teachers Association, International House, 76 Bennett Road, Brighton, East Sussex BN2 5JL. Tel: 01273 685652, fax: 01273 674388, website: www.idta.co.uk, email: info@idta.co.uk

International ISRC Agency, c/o International Federation of the Phonographic Industry, 54 Regent Street, London W1B 5RE. Tel: 020 7878 7900, fax: 020 7878 7950, website: www.ifpi.org/isrc

London Disability Arts Forum for performers, 34 Osnaburgh Street, London NW1 3ND. Tel: 020 7916 5484, website: www.ldaf.net, email: enquiries@dail.dircom.co.uk

MCPS Mechanical Copyright Protection Society, collects and distributes royalties generated from recordings in many different formats. Website: www.mcps.co.uk

Metier Sector Training Organisation, established by and for the arts and entertainment sector to support training and personal development. Metier has: a database of consultants and training providers, careers information designed for entrants to the profession, advice on funding sources for training. Members are those working or wishing to work in arts and entertainment. Also publishes the *Arts Training Journal*. Glyde House, Glydegate, Bradford BD5 0BQ. Tel: 01274 738800, fax: 01274 391566, website: www.metier.org.uk, email: admin@mcticr.org.uk

The Musicians Network Looking for the 'right' musician, band, session work or just to jam. A database containing details on musicians of all instruments, styles, influences etc. (including photos), MN matches up the requirements of both parties. Register your own details or search for specific musicians with the MN. Membership costs £20.

Music Producers' Guild Organisation for anyone who is involved in the production of music and sound in all its forms. Regular meetings, equipment demonstrations and studio visits, legal and financial advice, discounts. Website: www.mpg.org.uk

Musicians' Union is a trade union for all musicians in the UK offering services (including career advice), benefits, assistance and advice and representing the musicians at industrial tribunals. Guidelines for gigging abroad (foreign contracts can also be vetted free). Members also get discounted rates for purchasing music, instruments and equipment. There are 73 regional branches with six specialist areas of music: session musicians, British Music Writers' Council, freelance orchestral, folk, roots and traditional music, jazz and theatre. 60/62 Clapham Road, London SW9 0JJ. Tel: 020 7582 5566, fax: 020 7582 9805, website: www.musiciansunion.org.uk, email: info@musiciansunion.org.uk

Music Publishers Association promotes and protects the interests of music publishers and assists publishers and composers in maximising their income. 3rd Floor, Strandgate, 18–20 York Building, London WC2N 6JU. Tel: 020 7839 7779, fax: 020 7839 7776, website: www.mpaonline.org.uk email: info@mpaonline.org.uk

NAYT: National Association of Youth Theatres has a national database of around 500 active youth theatre groups. Arts Centre, Vane Terrace, Darlington, County Durham DL3 7AX. Tel: 01325 363330, website: www.nayt.org.uk, email: naytuk@aol.com

NCDT: National Council for Drama Training is particularly concerned with linking together those engaged in training and those working in the profession. For information on training and a list of accredited courses, contact: 5 Tavistock Place, London WC1H 9SS. Tel: 020 7387 3650, fax: 020 7681 4733, website: www.ncdt.co.uk, email: info@ncdt.co.uk

NDAF: National Disability Arts Forum Disability as a political art form, promoting equality of opportunity for disabled people in all aspects of the arts. Weekly newspage, *Etcetera*, which includes job opportunities, website information and arts and disabilities opportunities. Mea House, Ellison Place, Newcastle NE1 8XS. Tel: 0191 261 1628, textphone: 0191 261 2237, website: www.ndaf.org, email ndaf@ndaf.org

National Music and Disability Information Service See Sound Sense below.

NRCD: National Resource Centre for Dance supports the development of dance study, publishes materials, runs short courses with an archive and reference collection. University of Surrey, Guildford, Surrey GU2 5XH. Tel: 01483 259316, website: www.surrey.ac.uk/NRCD, email: nrcd@surrey.ac.uk

National Youth Arts Wales Represents the National Youth Brass Band/Choir/Chamber Ensemble/Dance/Orchestra and Theatre of Wales. Workshops, training and performance opportunities. 245 Western Avenue, Cardiff CF5 2YX. Tel: 029 2026 5060, fax: 029 2026 5014, website: www.nyaw.co.uk, email: nyaw@nyaw.co.uk

The Place Dance Services Dancers can contact this service for information and advice as well as professional support and artist development – degree, summer, professional and evening courses. They also have a huge database of dancers nationally and internationally, and publish a newsletter for members called *Juice*, which amongst other things gives information on auditions and jobs. They can also advise on how to set up your own dance company and how to approach promoters etc. The Place Dance Services run a membership scheme – one of the largest groups of members is students who can progress through the structure as they graduate. 17 Duke's Road, London WC1 9PY. Tel: 020 7383 3524, fax: 020 7388 5407, website: www.theplace.org.uk, email: artistdevelopment@theplace.org.uk

PRS: Performing Rights Society 29-33 Berners Street, London W1T 3AB. Tel: 020 7306 4804, fax: 020 7306 4350, website: www.prs.co.uk

RADA: The Royal Academy of Dramatic Art 62-64 Gower Street, London WC1E 6ED. Tel: 020 7636 7076, website: www.rada.org email: enquiries@rada.ac.uk

RNIB: Royal National Institute for the Blind 105 Judd Street, London WC1H 9NE. Tel: 020 7388 1266, website: www.rnib.org.uk, email: rnib@rnib.org.uk

Royal Academy of Dancing 36 Battersea Square, London SW11 3RA. Tel: 020 7326 8000, website: www.rad.org.uk, email: info@rad.org.uk

RSA Examinations Board, Progress House, Westwood Way, Coventry CV4 8JQ. Website: www.ocv.org.uk, email: cib@ocv.org.uk

SAC: Scottish Arts Council funds (through an annual government grant) Scottish artists and art organisations supporting theatres, art centres, touring companies, contemporary dance and so on. 12 Manor Place, Edinburgh EH3 7DD. Tel: 0131 225 9833, website: www.sac.org.uk, email: help.desk@scottisharts.org.uk

Scottish Community Drama Association Works to promote all aspects of community theatre in Scotland and supports individuals and theatre clubs in the following areas: festivals, advice and training, information, play-writing and play libraries. Its quarterly magazine *Scene*, gives news of people and events in community theatre around Scotland and beyond. National Office, 5 York Place, Edinburgh EH1 3EB. Tel/fax: 0131 557 5552, website: www.scda.org.uk, email: headquarters@scda.org.uk

SBTD: Society of British Theatre Designers Access to an international network of designers, assistant designers, information on training courses throughout the UK, slide library, publications and participation in SBTD exhibitions – student membership available. 47 Bermondsey Street, London SE1 3XT. Tel: 020 7403 3778, fax: 020 7378 6170. website: www.theatredesign.org.uk

SCUDD: Standing Conference of University Drama Departments Website details on the 40+ university and college of higher education departments in its membership. Website: www.leeds.ac.uk/theatre/scudd

Skillset Sector Skill Council: 103 Dean Street, London W1D 3TH. Tel: 020 7534 5300, website: www.skillset.org, email: info@skillset.org

Society of Teachers of Speech and Drama gives advice and assistance to those who wish to train as teachers in speech, drama and communication and also provides support to teaching members. 73 Berry Hill Road, Mansfield NG18 4RU. Tel: 01623 627636, website: www.stsd.org.uk, email: ann.p.jones@btinternet.com

Sound Sense, national development agency for community music. Ensuring equal opportunity to participate in music, particularly for those who are normally excluded whether for social, physical or technical reasons. 7 Tavern Street, Stowmarket, Suffolk IP14 1PJ. Tel: 01449 673990, fax: 01449 673994, website: www.soundsense.org, email: info@soundsense.org

USEFUL ADDRESSES

Action Space runs London-wide arts events (and works with project workers who run the events) for people with learning disabilities in music, drama, dance, the media and arts in general. Tel: 020 7627 8855, website: www.actionspace.org, email: office@actionspace.org

Adzido Pan-African Dance Ensemble For information on productions, evening classes in African dance/drumming, education and community work or to join the mailing list contact Canonbury Business Centre, 202 New North Road, London N1 7BL. Tel: 020 7359 7453, website: www.adzido.com email: info@adzido.co.uk

CandoCo Contemporary dance company. Performance, education and integration – workshops with disabled and non-disabled people. 2L Leroy House, 436 Essex Road, London N1 3QP. Tel: 020 7704 6845, website: www.candoco.co.uk, email:info@candoco.co.uk

Calouste Gulbenkian Foundation 98 Portland Place, London W1B 1ET. Tel: 020 7636 5313, website: www.gulbenkian.org.uk, email: info@gulbenkian.org.uk

Channel 4 124 Horseferry Road, London SW1P 2TX. Tel: 020 7396 4444, website: www.channel4.com, email: viewerenquiries@channel4.com

Dance Books Publishes and retails books, CDs and videos on dance and human movement. The Old Bakery, 4 Lenten Street, Alton, Hampshire GU34 1HG. Tel: 01420 86138, website: www.dancebooks.co.uk, email: dl@dancebooks.co.uk

Drake Music Project Committed to providing opportunity for disabled people to explore, compose and perform their own music using specialist technology.

Edexcel Stewart House, 32 Russell Square, London WC1B 5DN. Tel: 0870 240 9800, website: www.edexcel.org.uk, email: enquiries@edexcel.org.uk

Generator Dedicated to supporting popular music community in NE England. Info and databases: media/A&R contacts, music facilities/businesses, support organisations, touring information packs by region – including *When Will I be Famous?* a guide to becoming a pop star and how to write a press release. Black Swan Court, 69 Westgate Road, Newcastle NE1 1SG. Tel: 0191 245 0099, fax: 0191 245 0144, website: www.generator.org.uk, email: mail@generator.org.uk

Graeae Theatre Company Runs training courses for disabled people, etc. For information on forthcoming productions join their mailing list. Hampstead Town Hall, 213 Haverstock Hill, London NW3 4QP. Tel: 020 7681 4755, fax: 020 7681 4755, textphone: 020 7681 4757, website: www.graeae.org email: info@graeae.org

International Dance Teachers' Association Information for potential performers and teachers – training, guidance and support. International House, 76 Bennett Road, Brighton, East Sussex BN2 5JL. Tel: 01273 685652, fax: 01273 685652, website: www.idta.co.uk, email: info@idta.co.uk

Laban Centre An institution for professional vocational training and also a centre for scholarly and creative research. *Dance Theatre Journal* and Laban Centre Working Papers in Dance Studies are published at the Laban Centre and it is home to Transitions Dance Company, South East London Youth Dance Company. Laurie Grove, London SE14 6NH. Tel: 020 8692 4070, website: www.laban.co.uk email: info@laban.co.uk

Londondance.com Ebulletin of dance, news special offers and job vacancies, news, directories menu, London dance companies, venues, organisations, classes, workshops, photographers, publications, dancers' health and more plus what's on.

National Film and Television School Beaconsfield Studios, Station Road, Beaconsfield, Bucks HP9 1LG. Tel: 01494 671234, fax: 01494

674042, website: www.nftsfilm-tv.ac.uk, email: admin@nftsfilm-tv.ac.uk

National Star Centre Innovative programmes for young people with physical disabilities including performing arts. Ullenwood, Cheltenham, Glos GL53 9QU. Tel: 01242 527631, website: www.natstar.ac.uk

NSTC: National Student Theatre Aims to give students and first year graduates who are prospective theatre professionals valuable experience of an extended run with a talented theatre group. They have had more than 100 Edinburgh Fringe Festival productions. Open to any current student or previous year's graduate welcome to apply to act. Graduates of more than 12 weeks may apply for any non-acting positions, especially director, producer, publicity manager, company manager or to assist in any of these areas. Check website for positions needed or look for audition ad in *The Stage*. Prospective directors with or without projects), producers, publicity personnel and administrators can apply at any time.

Orange Tree Theatre 1 Clarence Street, Richmond, Surrey TW9 2SA. Fax: 020 8332 0369, website: www.orangetreetheatre.co.uk, email: admin@orangetree.demon.co.uk

Shape London opens up access to the arts, enabling greater participation by disabled and older people. It runs arts workshops, projects and events in a variety of settings; NVQ, certificate and diploma Arts Management courses, short training courses and placements for disabled people. There is a national Deaf Arts Programme and Ticket Scheme with reduced price tickets and volunteer drivers for disabled and older people. 356 Holloway Road, London N7 6PA. Tel: 020 7619 6160, website: www.shapearts.org.uk, email: info@shapearts.org.uk

Society for Promotion of New Music From contemporary jazz, classical and pop to music for film, dance and other creative medias, SPNM is one of the main advocates of new music in the UK. 4th floor, 18-20 Southwark Street, London SE1 1TJ. Tel: 020 7404 1640, website: www.spnm.org.uk

Theatre Dance UK is a British Council website with In Profile, a directory of UK theatre and dance. See British Council website: http://theatredance.britishcouncil.org

UK Theatre Web Information on amateur groups, companies, organisations, people, venues and performance listings, *What's on Stage* and finding work in the performing arts industry. Website: www.uktw.co.uk/jobs.htm

Vocaleyes Britain's foremost audio description service for touring theatre and leading West End productions and pantomimes. Established through a grant from the National Lottery via the Arts Council of England. 25 Short Street, London SE1 8LJ. Website: www.vocaleyes.co.uk, email: enquiries@vocaleyes.co.uk

Recruitment

Career Moves secretarial employment agency for the music and media industries for temporary and permanent vacancies. Sutherland House, 5–6 Argyll Street, London W1V 1AD. Tel: 020 7292 2900, website: www.cmoves.co.uk, email: career@cmoves.ac.uk

Focus Management Limited in association with Bak Management. 155 Park Road, Teddington TW11 0BP Tel: 020 8241 2446, email: focus.mgt@virgin.net

Handle secretarial and senior temporary and permanent vacancies 4 Giles Court, London W1U 1JD. Tel: 020 7569 9999, website: www.handle.co.uk, email: info@handle.co.uk

Regional Arts Online Join to get arts jobs and arts news. An information service for the arts and cultural sector, established by the ten Regional Arts Boards (RABs) which covers the whole of England. A place where artists, arts organisations and adminstrators can communicate, share information and work together including Arts Jobs – current vacancies in the arts. Website: www.arts.org.uk/bb/arts-jobs/maillist/htm

Publishers

A&C Black 37 Soho Square, London W1D 3QZ. Website: www.acblack.com, email: publicity@acblack.com

AGCAS Information Booklets CSU Ltd, Prospect House, Booth Street East, Manchester M13 9EP. Website: www.prospects.ac.uk, email: enquiries@prospects.ac.uk

Arts Publishing International Unit A 402 Tower Bridge Business Complex, 100 Clements Road, London SE16 4DG. Tel: 020 7232 5803, fax: 020 7394 8753, website: www.api.co.uk, email: postmaster@api.co.uk

Dance Books – see Useful Addresses, above

Dancing Times Ltd 45-47 Clerkenwell Green, London EC1R 0EB. Tel: 020 7250 3006, website: www.dancing-times.co.uk, email: dt@dancing-times.co.uk

Hobson's Publishers 159-173 St John Street, London EC1V 4DR. Tel: 020 7958 5000, website: www.hobsons.com

IPC Media King's Reach Tower, Stamford Street, London SE1 9LF. Tel: 020 7261 5000, website: www.ipcmedia.co.uk, email: name@ipcmedia.co.uk

Oxford University Press Great Clarendon Street, Oxford OX2 6DP. Tel: 01865 556767, website: www.oup.co.uk

Phaidon Press Ltd Regent's Wharf, All Saints Street, London N1 9PA. Tel: 020 7843 1000, website: www.phaidon.com

Rhinegold Publishing 241 Shaftesbury Avenue, London WC2H 8TF. Tel: 020 7333 1721, website: www.rhinegold.co.uk

Richmond House Publishing Ltd Douglas House, 3 Richmond Buildings, London W1D 3HE. Tel: 020 7437 9556, fax: 020 7287 3463, email: sales@rhpco.co.uk

Showcase Publications Hollis Publishing Ltd, Harlequin House, 7 High Street, Teddington, Middlesex TW11 6EL. Tel: 020 8977 7711, website: www.showcase-music.com, email: showcase@hollis-pr.com

Trotman and Co Ltd 2 The Green, Richmond, Surrey TW9 1PL. Tel: 020 8486 1150, fax 020 8486 1161, website: www.careers-portal.co.uk email: mail@trotman.co.uk

Virgin Books Thames Wharf Studios, Rainville Road, London W6. Tel: 020 7386 3300, website: www.virginbooks.com email: info@virgin-books.co.uk